# THE MIRACLE EQUATION

# THE MIRACLE EQUATION

## The Two Decisions That Move
## Your Biggest Goals from
## Possible, to Probable, to Inevitable

# HAL ELROD

**HARMONY**
BOOKS · NEW YORK

Copyright © 2019 by Hal Elrod

All rights reserved.
Published in the United States by Harmony Books,
an imprint of the Crown Publishing Group,
a division of Penguin Random House LLC, New York.
crownpublishing.com

Harmony Books is a registered trademark, and the Circle colophon is a
trademark of Penguin Random House LLC.

Library of Congress Cataloging-in-Publication Data
Names: Elrod, Hal, 1979– author.
Title: The miracle equation / Hal Elrod.
Description: New York : Harmony Books, [2019]
Identifiers: LCCN 2018058103 | ISBN 9781984823700 (hardcover) |
ISBN 9781984823724 (ebook)
Subjects: LCSH: Self-realization. | Self-actualization (Psychology)
Classification: LCC BF637.S4 E4455 2019 | DDC 158.1—dc23
LC record available at https://lccn.loc.gov/2018058103

ISBN 978-1-9848-2370-0
Ebook ISBN 978-1-9848-2372-4

Printed in the United States of America

Book design by Andrea Lau
Jacket design by Pete Garceau

10 9 8 7 6 5 4 3 2 1

First Edition

This book is dedicated to the people whom my heart belongs to and my world revolves around—my family.

Ursula, my wife for life, your love and support make everything I do possible (including this book). I adore you.

Sophie and Halsten, you are my favorite miracles.
My mission in life is to be the best father I can possibly be for you.

I love you all more than I (or any author) could ever put into words.

# CONTENTS

# BEFORE WE BEGIN

messed up with my last book, *The Miracle Morning.*

My goal was to *change one million lives, one morning at a time.* I took that goal seriously. It took more than eighteen months of non-stop promotion to hit a wave of momentum and more than five years to reach that goal, but the book did eventually make it into the hands of more than one million people who needed it. To get there, I was interviewed on hundreds of podcasts, did more than a dozen television interviews, filled my speaking engagement calendar, and created a Facebook community so I could interact with readers directly, all to light a beacon for those looking to better themselves with a simple yet highly effective daily personal development practice.

From the outside, it looked as though I had achieved that goal. If you are one of the more than one million people who have read that book, joined the Miracle Morning Community on Facebook, or been impacted by someone in the previous two camps, you may be scratching your head and wondering *How can a book and a message that have reached—and seemingly helped—so many people not be considered a success?* I know. It took me a while to accept this perspective myself. I mean, by all measurements, I had achieved my goal.

The Miracle Morning is now practiced daily by hundreds of thousands of people in more than one hundred countries. I receive messages daily from people with stories of miraculous health recoveries (from cancer survivors to accident victims), many pounds shed, books written, and new businesses started. People have moved, traveled, and found love. Generally speaking, the Miracle Morning has supported countless people to discover and share their own unique gifts, which makes the world better for all of us.

All of these wins fill my heart with tremendous gratitude.

Still, something had been nagging at me since that book was published in 2012. Though having a committed daily personal development practice is what will enable you to develop the internal qualities and characteristics you need to achieve everything you want in your life, it doesn't actually produce achievements. It's only half of the equation, so to speak. You can meditate every day, read personal development books, gain clarity by journaling, and become the most knowledgeable, confident, and prepared person you could ever be—and then do nothing. How helpful is that?

Maybe this scenario sounds familiar to you. Your bookshelves are overflowing with more wisdom than you have time to read, or you are a regular at "how to transform your life" lectures and conferences. Still, you feel as though something is missing. The results just aren't there. Your bank account isn't where you want it to be. The personal relationship that you're in and that you expected to be so fulfilling . . . isn't. Maybe you are struggling to start or build a business, find a career that suits you, or just find happiness in your everyday life. Or maybe all of the above *has* happened, yet you are still driven to attain that elusive *next* level of personal or professional success.

If you have found yourself in this situation (and trust me, I've been guilty of it myself), you may well be (probably unknowingly) part of an overflowing group of "personal development junkies." Speaking as a recovering member, I know we love the high of those Ah-ha! moments, and that's what we chase. But nothing ever really changes. No lasting transformation occurs. We just continue on, persistently wanting the same things. I used to devour book after book, believing that with each new morsel of wisdom I absorbed, I became a better version of myself. As if just that knowledge, tucked safely inside my brain, were sufficient. It's not uncommon to think that engaging in daily personal development is enough in and of itself. But it's not. If you're sick of setting goals only to beat yourself up for not achieving them, you are not alone (and you will also get a lot out of this book).

You must follow your daily personal development practice with a proven process to set and achieve meaningful goals that will consistently improve the quality of your life. I still remember the day I stopped, looked at my life, and realized *I can do more. I can be more. And I'm no longer willing to settle.* I had basically coasted through my younger years, putting in the smallest amount of effort necessary to get the greatest return, and I was no longer okay with that. So I began actively moving toward my biggest goals, instead of expecting (more like hoping) that they would come to me if I could just visualize them clearly enough in my mind. Over time, I developed a process that translates the synthesis of all that personal development knowledge into action. I realized that from that action, which is oftentimes simple and quite ordinary, extraordinary results will emerge.

If you are a regular in the personal development world, you've already heard that *anything is possible.* And I do believe that. Yet *possible* isn't enough to get you out of bed in the morning fueled with the internal motivation to tackle your biggest dreams. I wish it were, but it's not. Offering a halfway-there plan wasn't enough. With my next book—this book—I wanted to create something that would help move your success from *possible* to *probable* and eventually to *inevitable.*

The Miracle Equation is that process. As you'll learn, the Miracle Equation is deceptively simple to explain but only a small percentage of our society understand how to execute it. It consists of only two decisions:

The first decision is to maintain *Unwavering Faith* and the second is to put forth *Extraordinary Effort,* and the key to creating tangible, measurable miracles is to do both, over an extended period of time.

When we study the world's most prolific achievers, innovators, philanthropists, athletes, and just about anyone else who has made a significant contribution to the world, we see that they have done so by establishing and maintaining Unwavering Faith that they could and then putting forth Extraordinary Effort until they did. When you consistently maintain Unwavering Faith and put forth Extraordinary Effort over an extended period of time, you cannot fail. You may stumble, you may experience setbacks, but your success will ultimately move from possible . . . to probable . . . to inevitable.

At the point of being able to make reaching your goals inevitable is where you become what I call a *Miracle Maven*. Miracle Mavens have solved the mystery of creating miracles and live by the Miracle Equation. Unwavering Faith is their de facto mindset. Extraordinary Effort is how they approach all of their goals. Committed to these two decisions, Miracle Mavens create extraordinary results in the world, not just for themselves but for everyone. And because miracles are their way of life, they consistently create extraordinary results over and over again, in nearly everything they do. Embodying the qualities and characteristics of a Miracle Maven is the ultimate goal and where you will land after you read and implement the strategies in this book.

## THE MOST EFFECTIVE WAY TO READ THIS BOOK

I know that some personal development books can be read piecemeal. You can skip around and read the chapters at will and out of order. I know some folks who close their eyes, open their book to a random page, and then read that chapter. Those books give you, the reader, control over what you think will be important to you each time you pick up the book. Those books are great. But this book isn't like that.

The first two chapters, in addition to this introduction, lay the foundation for creating tangible, measurable miracles. We will discuss what miracles are (and are not), then look at an overview of the Miracle Equation and how the two decisions, Unwavering Faith and Extraordinary Effort, feed into each other and make this process easier and easier over time. We'll then look at the story of my first miracle and how I came to put together this equation just before my twenty-second birthday and how I began teaching it to one person after another, watching (somewhat in awe) as it worked for them, just as it had worked for me.

The remainder of this book walks you through the concepts and steps you need to understand before you create miracles on your own. We'll cover

- How to overcome the internal conflict between your limitations (from which we all suffer) and your innate limitless potential

- How to develop emotional invincibility so that you remain in control of your emotions no matter what life sends your way (this strategy is really helpful to remember when you think your efforts aren't producing adequate results)

- The real purpose of setting a goal

- How to choose your first (and subsequent) miracle to create

- How to keep creating miracles over and over again

- How to put all of this information into practice with your own Miracle Equation 30-Day Challenge to start you on your path to creating your first tangible, measurable miracle

I would encourage you to read this book all the way through from front to back the first time because the chapters build on one another. You will want to understand the material in each chapter before continuing. After your first read-through, feel free to pick and choose the chapters you would like to revisit at any point. I would especially encourage you to read chapters again if you find yourself stuck in the midst of creating a miracle.

## A FEW THINGS TO REMEMBER AS YOU READ THIS BOOK

**1. The Miracle Morning and the Miracle Equation can work together.** If you have not read *The Miracle Morning*, don't panic. Reading this book alone will provide you the tools necessary to capitalize on more of your potential and create a more fulfilling life. You will learn how to achieve extraordinary, measurable results (miracles) again and again, and eventually with relative ease. That said, the Miracle Morning does help you gain clarity, calm, and focus before you start your day. It might not be quite as results oriented, but it is a proven daily personal development practice that will help you become the person you need to be to achieve your goals.

**2. Several concepts are repeated throughout.** The Miracle Equation is simple to explain but a little more complex to execute. So I don't introduce any concept just once and leave it at that. Instead, I revisit crucial concepts throughout the book on purpose and often in different ways to help you internalize and remember what matters most. It's much easier to retain information that you have seen several times.

**3. My intention with this book is to elevate the consciousness of humanity, one person at a time.** As I mentioned at the start of this introduction, my intention with *The Miracle Morning* was to change one million lives, one morning at a time. Once a million lives were changed for the better, I realized that that once seemingly unrealistic and impossible goal was not only realistic, it was not big enough.

With this book, my intention is to elevate the consciousness of humanity, one person at a time. That may sound pretty lofty to you now (you may even have rolled your eyes). But after reading this book, you'll realize that there is no vision too big. As we each begin to tap into our unlimited potential, our own consciousness is elevated, which influences and elevates the consciousness of those around us.

And as we begin creating tangible, measurable miracles, those results also impact everyone who is affected by them. I invite you, as you read, to set your own intention through the understanding that *you are limitless and destined to have, be, and create whatever you decide.* What gaps do you see in the world around you? What contribution do you believe (or maybe half believe) you can make? What, for you, is the ultimate miracle? I promise, no goal will be out of your reach.

Now let's get started. Our first lesson involves taking the mystery out of miracles.

I

# TAKING THE MYSTERY OUT OF MIRACLES

Moving from Mythical to Measurable

Miracles are not contrary to nature,
but only contrary to
what we know about nature.

—SAINT AUGUSTINE

M iracles. They're kinda *mysterious*, right? I mean, isn't that part of the appeal, not knowing exactly how certain seemingly imperceptible events have lined up perfectly to save someone's life or deliver their wildest dream right to their front door? However, this mysterious nature also creates a problem with the way that we perceive miracles.

I once saw a segment on the *Today* show titled "Skydiving Miracle: Man Falls Two Miles" about skydiving instructor Michael Holmes, who fell 14,000 feet when his parachute failed to open. As the ground below raced toward him, he tried to release the parachute but couldn't. He tried to cut it free, but that didn't work, either. In a last-ditch effort to save his own life, he pulled the reserve parachute, but it didn't release. In the final seven hundred feet that he spent free-falling through the air, he resigned himself to dying. Amazingly, he didn't die. Relatively speaking, his injuries were fairly minor.

And have you heard Donnie Register's story? It was all over the news as "Donnie's Miracle," and Oprah.com even featured it as a "Real-Life Miracle." Donnie was standing behind the cash register in his own antique store when a gunman fired a shot at his head. Donnie threw his hands up in front of his face. The bullet bounced off Donnie's gold wedding band, which deflected the shot, and he miraculously dodged what should have been sudden death.

Over the years, I've heard of miraculous health recoveries, where there seemed to be no other effort made except heavy doses of hope. And even of long-lost sweethearts who mysteriously crossed paths decades after they parted ways. All of these stories are intriguing and awe-inducing at the same time.

In all fairness, stories like these can be called miracles. But for many folks (and you may be one of them), it's miracles like these that give all miracles a bad name. Miracle nonbelievers assume that extraordinary events happen only to other people. They believe that all miracles are elusive. Mythical. Random. Lucky. And out of reach. Totally unrealistic and unpredictable. They just don't happen in real life—not to them, at least. I used to feel the same way.

I mean, if we could simply "think up" a seven-figure check to be waiting for us in our mailbox, wouldn't everyone be a millionaire? Miraculous health recoveries would be the norm, and that difficult client or coworker—you know, the one who's constantly spiking your blood pressure—would . . . well, he or she might just disappear. If you fall into this camp, you probably think that you have to see it to believe it.

Being skeptical can be a good thing. You're doing what we should all be doing; thinking critically, evaluating and questioning everything, going in search of the truth. I approach things the same way and don't expect anything less from you.

However, there is a potentially devastating downside to skepticism that we all need to be aware and cautious of: it can easily turn into cynicism. It can tip us into an unhealthy level of distrust and limit the possibilities that are otherwise available to us. As you'll learn in this book, there are actually two different types of miracles, and it's not really fair or beneficial to blend them together.

The miracles that we've described above are what you might call "passive" or "random" miracles, those that occur by chance. We marvel at their unbelievable nature, but there is no definitive way to explain them, let alone repeat them (and I'm sure that that skydiving instructor and Donnie Register would prefer not to endure their experiences again). They can be seen as random coincidences. If you would like to create these kinds of miracles, which often include a "pray and wait" approach, I'm sorry, but I don't have much advice for you. They are not the kinds of miracles we will be discussing in this book.

This book *is* about the kind of tangible, measurable miracles that require your active participation in producing them. They are more akin to making your biggest, scariest, and most improbable goals come true. These are the types of miracles that you have a significant degree of control over, meaning that you can consistently create them again and again in your life because you will understand how the process works. But to create this kind of miracle, first you must believe that the result you are seeking is possible and that *you* can produce it. If you fell into the skeptics' group above, I would urge you to suspend your disbelief for a moment so that you can explore what else might be possible for you. At least while you read this book.

Now, don't get me wrong; I'm not trying to convince you to believe something unreasonable. What I am trying to do is open your mind to the possibility of something new, a second kind of miracle that you have the power to create at will. In this chapter, we will define what tangible, measurable miracles are, for the purposes of our conversation, and then dive into exactly how these types of miracles unfold so that you, too, can create uncommon results. Then it will be up to you if you want to believe.

## ANYONE CAN CREATE TANGIBLE, MEASURABLE MIRACLES

When it comes to miracles, there are some questions that would be helpful for us to consider, such as Are miracles experienced only by special or "chosen" individuals? Do miracles occur only at random? Are miracles created by God or some other mysterious higher intelligence? Or could it be that we were each born with a limitless potential and capabilities far greater than what we believe about ourselves? What if that's why some people are wildly successful—because they've figured out how to tap into the dormant potential that every single one of us was born with? What if you realized that you're only a decision (or two) away from tapping into that potential?

A realization like this would change the way you approach the size and scope of the goals you're willing to set and the life you live. It would raise the bar on what it means to be "average," if average were to become extraordinary. Imagine if you and every person you know began actualizing his or her full potential, if each of us were to discover how to overcome our self-imposed limitations and begin creating everything we want for our lives while making a profound impact in the world. What if we all became Miracle Mavens?

## WHAT IS A MIRACLE MAVEN?

The word *maven* comes from the Yiddish word *meyvn* and the Hebrew word *mebhin*, meaning "one who understands."

Though the word *miracle* has several definitions, the most useful one for us as we move forward, found in the *English Oxford Living Dictionary*, is "a remarkable event or development that brings very welcome consequences."

Miracle Mavens encompass these two definitions in one body.

If you were to think about it, I'm sure you could come up with a few people who are living close to their full potential and seem to have a knack for bringing their visions into reality. Whether you know them personally or admire them from afar, these individuals never let anyone (including themselves) talk them out of their grand ideas. They seem to have an unlimited well of creativity and perseverance. Opportunities abound for these folks. You may wonder how or why they're always so lucky. But what if luck played only a teeny-tiny part in their overall success, if at all?

Throughout history, there have been many people who actively created tangible, measurable miracles. US president John F. Kennedy, who envisioned putting a man on the moon, and the civil rights leader Martin Luther King, Jr., who imagined a free and equal America for all people, are examples of individuals who intentionally and actively created miracles. While others prayed and waited for those results to happen, JFK and MLK went out and made them happen. They succeeded in transforming seemingly impossible ideas into tangible reality. They followed their visions as far as they could and in doing so created extraordinary new realities. By tapping into their abilities, they became Miracle Mavens.

Because becoming a Miracle Maven is just that—a way of being. When you live with Unwavering Faith and put forth Extraordinary Effort, you are a Miracle Maven. Notable Miracle Mavens come from all walks of life, and their accomplishments—and the pathways they forged—come in every imaginable permutation. Many you know simply because their accomplishments have made such a significant impact on our world. Well-known Miracle Mavens include

- Henry Ford, who gave us transportation by car

- Marie Curie, who developed the theory of radioactivity and was the first woman to win a Nobel Prize and the first person to be granted that prestigious award twice

- Bill Gates, who put personal computers into millions of homes and offices around the world

- Amelia Earhart, the first woman to fly solo across the Atlantic Ocean

- Neil Armstrong, who walked on the moon

- LeBron James, who gave the city of Cleveland a miracle when he led the Cavaliers to win the city's first championship in a major professional sport in more than sixty years

- Michael Phelps, who became an Olympian at age fifteen and went on to win twenty-three gold medals

- Steve Jobs, who put thousands of songs into our pockets and made smartphones the norm

- Elon Musk, who is constantly creating technological miracles that help move humanity forward

From the beginning of time, otherwise ordinary people have catapulted themselves beyond the limits of what was thought to be possible. They, too, have had to overcome the same types of fears and insecurities that chain us all. We are all born with unlimited potential, but these people have figured out how to tap into it. When you discover how to do the same, everything changes.

Though the circumstances that each of us were born into vary from person to person, the unlimited human potential that each of us is born with is universal. In fact, there are countless stories of individuals who were born into challenging conditions yet found a way to turn their lives into something extraordinary. You may be familiar with some of them.

The author J. K. Rowling was broke and nearly destitute when she wrote the first *Harry Potter* book, which ultimately turned into a series—and several blockbuster movies, theme park rides, toys, clothing, video games, and more—and secured her spot in the exclusive billionaires' club.

Jay-Z grew up poor in a Brooklyn housing project before moving on to become a world-famous rapper and business tycoon. His empire includes real estate, sports bars, clothing, beverages, and even beauty products, just to name a few.

Oprah Winfrey had a childhood filled with poverty and abuse and became one of the most successful and wealthy women in the world. Now, with a commitment to paying her success forward and helping future generations make their way out of poverty, she has donated more than $150 million to charitable causes that help underprivileged girls.

The actor Sylvester Stallone was homeless for brief periods as he worked his way up from bit acting parts to his breakout role in *Rocky*, which he also wrote. The *Rocky* franchise went on to become one of the most successful of all time.

This list could continue with enough real-life examples to fill this entire book. What I hope you are realizing is that your external circumstances do not confine you, just as your past does not dictate your future. You will first need to envision your ideal future, see it clearly, and then establish the belief that it's possible. (We'll spend a lot of time discussing how to do exactly that in the coming pages.) Then you must begin to move toward it. That's what the folks listed above did. They decided that what they wanted was possible, figured out what they needed to do to make it probable, and then continued giving it everything they had until their success became inevitable. You can absolutely do the same.

Remember, the goal you decide to tackle does not necessarily have to be world changing. It can be as big or small, as easy or complicated, as you like. The key is that it must be meaningful to you. That significance will serve as your driver.

In *The Miracle Morning*, I described a concept called *Level 10 success*, which is simply the ideal that we all aspire to live. If you were to measure success in any area of your life on a scale of 1 to 10, you would likely want to be a 10 in every area. Level 10 health. Level 10 happiness. Level 10 wealth. You name it. However, since human potential is unlimited, the objective is not necessarily to reach Level 10. It's simply to wake up every day and invest time into becoming a better version of the person you were when you went to bed the night before. When you focus each day on leaning into your limitless potential and moving toward Level 10 success in every area of your life, opportunities will become abundant and you will discover the source of true fulfillment.

As we strive toward Level 10 success, the challenge is to find the balance between being happy and grateful and seeing the perfection of where we are now while following the innate human desire to grow and improve. The key is not to come from a place of *I'm not good enough* but rather from *I am limitless, and I have more to give.* It's a subtle yet radical difference. It's a difference that Miracle Mavens live by.

Miracle Mavens set themselves apart because they are always reaching for something higher than their definition of Level 10 success. They maintain an unwavering belief in themselves and expect that what they want in their life will come to be. But they don't take a passive role in their pursuits. They don't stare at a vision board or mindlessly repeat affirmations and then wonder why nothing is happening. When you live as a Miracle Maven, you think and act differently from the majority of people.

Whereas most people habitually allow their fear and self-doubt to consume their thinking, Miracle Mavens choose to override fear with faith. They have a foundational mindset that they can and will win at everything they do, while simultaneously being willing to accept when they don't win and quickly moving on. That way they can take advantage of more opportunities. Even if it means that they will fail some of the time, they still have more chances to win.

Simon Sinek expressed a similar sentiment when he said, "Champions are not the ones who always win races; champions are the ones who get out there and try. And try harder the next time. . . . 'Champion' is a state of mind. They are devoted. They compete to best themselves as much if not more than they compete to best others."

Miracle Mavens also behave differently. They understand that they must put forth effort to get results. They don't seek the easy way; they're willing to do what's necessary to earn what it is that they want. However, they also value efficiency, so they're always learning and figuring out tips, tricks, and even shortcuts to get them to their goal faster.

I know this not only from observation but from experience. In later pages, you'll read how I used the Miracle Equation to walk again after being pronounced dead in a car accident, turned my financial situation around after near collapse, and survived a dismal cancer prognosis. I did nothing more than make and maintain the two decisions this book is based on.

## CREATING MIRACLES IS YOUR DECISION

Self-help books have given us countless answers to what holds us back from the lives we want. It's our habits, our beliefs, our circle of influence, our level of confidence, our energy, the law of attraction, time management, emotional intelligence, our education or lack thereof. It's all a little overwhelming. However, I believe we can simplify hundreds of answers into two straightforward decisions that will make or break your success and determine whether you will live the rest of your life as a Miracle Maven.

There are two decisions that we consciously fail to make, over and over again, that hold us back from accomplishing what we want to. They are: the decision to maintain Unwavering Faith and the decision to put forth Extraordinary Effort. What prevents anyone from creating the life they truly want is that either they lack faith that they can or they don't put forth the necessary effort. That's it. And many people don't do either.

I realize that this sounds simple—maybe even too simple. But let's explore this.

**DECISION 1: Unwavering Faith.** Although you can call faith by another name—belief, confidence, or conviction—simply put, those who create extraordinary lives do so by establishing the faith that they can, and they continue to reinforce and maintain that faith until they create what they desire. Thus, their faith is *unwavering.*

This defies human nature, in which our faith tends to be influenced by our past and present results and circumstances. Establishing faith that you can overcome or accomplish something that you've never overcome or accomplished before requires you to venture outside your comfort zone. It requires that you see yourself as better than you've ever been and envision a possibility that may lack evidence that it's actually possible. Establishing such faith isn't normal or natural, and it certainly isn't automatic. Establishing faith in your most limitless capabilities requires a conscious, deliberate decision to do so.

Maintaining that faith isn't natural, either. Nearly all worthwhile accomplishments are obtained only after a myriad of obstacles and setbacks have been overcome. For many people, obstacles and setbacks cause their faith to waver and their pursuit of what they want to halt. Which leads us to the second decision that you will need to make to create miracles.

## THE MIRACLE EQUATION IN ACTION

Rob Dial was one of my first coaching clients back in 2006 and has since become a friend and colleague. He has used the Miracle Equation in a remarkable way not only to gain financial freedom but also to make a significant impact in the world.

Every year, my longtime friend and business partner, Jon Berghoff (whom you'll meet later in the book), and I host the Best Year Ever [Blueprint] live experience, an event that takes people through a revolutionary process that sets them up to ensure that the next twelve months of their life are literally the best twelve months of their life. It was during one of these events that Rob realized his purpose in life was to teach people how to free themselves from their own suffering that they had created by holding themselves back from reaching their true potential. Shortly after that realization, he started his first podcast and within eight weeks had more than 100,000 downloads. Rob was thrilled, but he still had a job he loved with a six-figure salary. He knew he couldn't do both, so he used his Unwavering Faith in himself and his mission to leave his job and focus full-time on his life's purpose.

He used Extraordinary Effort to figure out how to create content that people would love and share, and within fourteen months, he had grown a social media following to over one million people. In 2017 alone, his Facebook page had more than 500 million views of the videos and content that he had produced. As for the six-figure job he had left behind, he was able to replace his income within fourteen months and, in his second full year, he made 300 percent more than his previous yearly salary. Rob experienced firsthand what it means to apply the Miracle Equation and become a Miracle Maven.

**DECISION 2: Extraordinary Effort.** Though you can also find a variety of synonyms to replace effort—work, productivity, exertion, or action—ultimately those who achieve meaningful goals and live Level 10 lives do so by putting forth the necessary (and typically *extraordinary*) effort until they create their desired outcomes. You'll learn in a later chapter that Extraordinary Effort isn't necessarily hard work. But it does require energy on your part. What makes the effort *extraordinary* is that it is sustained over an extended period of time. And without it, you will have nothing to fuel your faith.

Unfortunately, this type of effort is also unnatural. We often choose short-term pleasure at the expense of long-term success and fulfillment. Doing so causes us to put forth the minimal amount of effort necessary to remain safe and within our comfort zone. It prevents us from doing what's right, since doing what's easy is so much—well—easier.

Human nature confines the majority of our society to circumstances such as earning enough money to keep from losing the roof over our head but not enough to get ahead. We eat foods chosen purely for their taste and texture that provide us with short-lived moments of pleasure while robbing us of a lifetime of vibrant health and energy. We hold on to jobs we find unfulfilling in companies that provide us with what we perceive to be a secure paycheck, instead of pursuing goals and dreams that could earn us a fortune and award us the financial freedom we all desire.

I do realize that I'm asking you to make two decisions that will run counter to your basic instincts. In case you're wondering how you're going to defy your inborn human nature, bear with me. We will cover how to overcome these instincts so that, in time, these decisions can become automatic and natural.

## THE UNWAVERING FAITH AND
## EXTRAORDINARY EFFORT FEEDBACK LOOP

We've all been there. We're all jazzed up about a new goal we've set. We have a clear vision in our mind of what it will look and feel like to accomplish this goal. We know exactly what we have to do to get there, and we believe that it's possible. We take our first steps and are cruising along. And then suddenly . . . *thud*.

We hit an obstacle we weren't expecting. Results aren't happening as quickly as we had hoped. Maybe no one is getting back to you on those résumés you sent out. Maybe your boss put you onto a new project just when you were planning to use your free time to work out or start your own blog. Maybe you've launched your new product, but the sales aren't rolling in at the rate you were expecting. It's at times like these that sticking with the Miracle Equation is challenging. The bigger the obstacle thrown in front of you, the more discouraged you might feel. This is when you are most vulnerable to throwing the equation out the window and going back to "life as you know it."

When you don't see the results you expect (i.e., want), it's natural to let your faith waver. As soon as you've lost your faith, the effort that is necessary to achieve your goal disappears right behind it. I'm sure you've asked yourself once or twice, What's the point in even trying when I simply don't believe that reaching my goal is likely?

Unwavering Faith and Extraordinary Effort each pulls its own weight, and they also support each other. Instead of viewing them as two distinct lines of action, it's more realistic to view them as a circle or a wheel. They work together. When you establish Unwavering Faith that you can reach a goal, you create the internal drive necessary to propel yourself into action, which is your Extraordinary Effort. That effort then feeds into a sense of deservingness that fuels more faith. When you are plugged into both, the equation works. But if you fall off track with one, the process will come to a grinding halt. They function as feedback for each other. When you approach your life, your goals, your dreams, and even your relationships with Unwavering Faith and you put forth Extraordinary Effort, you'll keep the feedback loop going. That's how you create miracles again and again. That is how you live your life as a Miracle Maven.

## PUTTING THE MYSTERY BACK INTO MIRACLES

I know, I know. We just took the mystery out of miracles. Well, now we're going to put a little back in. This is because when you actively override your fear and self-doubt with Unwavering Faith and release the unproductive habits or lazy tendencies that have been preventing you from putting forth Extraordinary Effort, you immediately tap into your full capabilities and start seeing opportunities and synchronicities all around you. Achieving what you set out to do will become second nature. From the outside looking in, it often looks like luck.

People observe Miracle Mavens with a sense of awe, and sometimes even envy, thinking, *Geez, everything just flows for them. They're so lucky!* People with strong religious or spiritual beliefs will likely attribute success to God or some other higher power. Skeptics will dismiss it as random coincidence.

Call it what you want, credit whomever you like, just don't question it. Embrace it. See the truth and the simplicity in it. And remember that when you set out to achieve a massive dream or create an extraordinary result (aka miracle), you can't know what the journey to get there will look like. Just know that it will include all sorts of unexpected paths, challenges, relationships, and lessons that will guide you to new opportunities, which will in turn teach you lessons that will lead to more new opportunities.

You can't predict when and how luck will show up for you. But you can rest assured that the more you live by the Miracle Equation, the luckier you will get. The more you're willing to put yourself out there and attempt to create miracles by putting forth Extraordinary Effort and maintaining Unwavering Faith over an extended period of time, the more unpredictable and invaluable resources will show up in your life. That's when people will start looking at *you* and thinking, *Geez, everything just flows for them. They're so lucky!*

I'm telling you from experience, both my own and that of all the people you're about to meet throughout this book, that when you live in alignment with the Miracle Equation, miracles—results beyond what you thought were possible—do begin to show up, and almost always in unexpected ways. Unseen forces and resources beyond your current realm of awareness, that you could never have predicted or planned for, come to your aid to cocreate each miracle. They often show up in the form of unexpected opportunities or people or simply being in the right place at the right time.

I hear your inner skeptic rising to the surface. *Come on, Hal, unseen forces and resources beyond our current realm of awareness?* I hear you. It does sound a little "out there." Even so, it's a leap you must take. It's the same leap that every Miracle Maven took at some point in his or her life, which is why we consistently hear successful people credit "luck" as playing a role in their success. Sometimes it is necessary to believe in what you cannot see. I invite you to have faith in the magic and the miracles of life, for only those who do get to experience them.

As I stated earlier, the Miracle Equation is simple to explain, but few people understand how to execute it. The two decisions, Unwavering Faith and Extraordinary Effort, are not complicated to understand, and when combined and sustained, they produce astounding outcomes. However, the execution of these two decisions is anything but straightforward, as both require that we consciously defy our natural tendencies, both inherent and learned. This is why only a relatively small percentage of our society understands how to apply this formula to create extraordinary results and why an even smaller group has been able to do so many times over.

It's this smaller group of Miracle Mavens that I'm inviting you to join, a group in which Unwavering Faith has become the default way of thinking and Extraordinary Effort has become ordinary and automatic. You now know the elements necessary to create a tangible, measurable miracle. It's up to you if you want to go further and understand how to apply them.

In the next chapter, I'm going to walk you through how I stumbled upon the Miracle Equation, created my very first tangible, measurable miracle, and began teaching others to do the same. Let's look at where and how this idea all began.

# 2

# FROM IMPOSSIBLE . . . TO IMPROBABLE . . . TO INEVITABLE

How I Discovered the Equation

If you want to experience
prosperity at a miraculous level,
you must leave behind your old ways
of thinking and develop a new way of
imagining what is possible for you
to experience in your life.

—DR. WAYNE DYER

know we're only on chapter 2, but I already have a confession to make: I didn't invent any miracle equation. This book could have been written centuries ago. Not by me, of course. I wasn't around back then. But it could have been penned by any other Miracle Maven. To clarify, I simply identified the formula and named what already was the Miracle Equation. In truth, this formula has been used throughout history by the world's most prolific creators and achievers, in all walks of life. They just didn't have a name for it.

When I was a kid watching my favorite basketball player, Michael Jordan, play for the Chicago Bulls, I never heard Coach Phil Jackson turn to his team in the fourth quarter and say, "Scottie [Pippen], you're going to get the ball to Michael. Michael, you'll fake left, then drive the lane, apply the Miracle Equation, and win the game!" Likewise, no one ever heard Martin Luther King, Jr., preach about using the Miracle Equation to advance the civil rights movement or read about how Elon Musk is using the equation to achieve his grand vision of building a life-sustaining city on Mars.

However, whether they realized it or not, the Miracle Equation is the formula that each of them used to achieve their extraordinary results. It is living in alignment with the equation that will enable you to tap into your ability to operate in any area of your life at a Level 10, too. It will be impossible not to.

The Miracle Equation was born out of my desire to hit a record-breaking sales goal at work that I thought was probably impossible but *really* wanted to achieve. I basically defied my natural tendency to take the easy road and instead bolted along the harder path. In the process, I learned one of the most valuable life lessons I have ever come across.

Let me set the scene for how the Miracle Equation came to be.

After college, I accepted a position as a sales representative for Cutco, selling high-end kitchen cutlery through in-home demonstrations. When I began, I had had no previous sales experience and was accustomed to living my entire life in the void between average and embarrassingly mediocre. I had been a C student, had never played organized sports, wasn't part of any clubs, was bullied in school, and held only one record, obtained at Yosemite High School, for the most hours of detention ever assigned to a student in a single school year. The total was 178 in case you were curious—not exactly an accomplishment that Mom and Dad were proud of.

With the support of and lessons from some incredible leaders and mentors at Cutco, a level of confidence (and competence) in myself began to emerge that had never existed before. I pushed myself to work harder. I attempted to achieve higher goals. Overall, I grew into someone who was a heck of a lot more capable than I had ever thought I could be and quickly became one of the company's top sales reps.

One way I stretched myself was by breaking sales records during push periods, which, in the Cutco world, are a fourteen-day sales contest during which the company fosters friendly competition within its sales force. This is done by incentivizing thousands of reps and managers with trophies and prizes, with the intention of bringing in record sales for the salesperson, his or her local office, and the company. It was during one of those push periods that the light bulb lit up for me and the Miracle Equation was born.

## THE PUSH PERIOD THAT BECAME A MIRACLE

In February 2001, at the age of twenty-one, I was coming off back-to-back $20,000 push periods, a feat that had been achieved by less than a handful of sales reps during the fifty-two-year history of the company. As the next push period approached, I was gearing up for my attempt to become the first sales rep ever to reach that $20,000 milestone three consecutive times.

It was ten in the morning when I walked into the Cutco sales office in Fremont, California, to turn in my orders for the prior week.

"My pal, Hal!" my sales manager, Frank Ordoubadi, said as he gave me an enthusiastic high five in the lobby. "You ready for this push period?"

My eyes widened as I took a deep breath, pursed my lips, and blew out an exaggerated exhalation. "I am . . . and I'm going for it, Frank. I'm going to try to set the record. I don't know how, but I've got to find a way to sell another $20,000 in the next fourteen days."

"Wow!" Frank gave me a wide smile. "You realize you'd be the first person to ever hit that mark three times, don't you!?"

I nodded my head yes. "I know. I'm super nervous."

Frank's face turned serious. "Now, you do realize that this push period is only ten days, right? Because of the conference being earlier, we don't have the full fourteen days."

I stared at Frank for a moment. "Please tell me you're joking."

"Sorry, Hal," he said with an I'm-sorry-I-have-to-tell-you-this face. "I thought you knew that."

"So, wait, does that mean that this won't technically count as a normal push period, like for records and rankings?" In that moment, I was desperately hoping to get a pass on the abbreviated push period so that I could attempt to set the record during the next full fourteen-day contest.

"No, unfortunately this push period counts just like the others."

My heart sank. I had spent the last few weeks wrapping my head around selling $20,000 in fourteen days, which was no easy feat. The idea of reaching the same goal in only ten days' time felt somewhere between pointless and impossible.

## A MIDDLE-OF-THE-NIGHT EPIPHANY

That night, I tossed and turned in bed while contemplating my options. Selling $20,000 in ten days was beyond anything I'd ever done before. I reasoned, *Maybe I should lower my goal to $15,000? $10,000? Or should I sit this one out?* Fear and self-doubt raced around inside my head. *How am I going to reach this goal?*

As my voice of self-doubt grew louder, clarity struck. I remembered a lesson that one of my mentors, Dan Casetta, had taught me, which he had learned from author and modern-day philosopher Jim Rohn. In my head I heard Dan's voice: "The purpose of a goal is not to reach the goal. The purpose of a goal is to become the type of person who can achieve any goal, by always giving it everything you have, regardless of your results. It's *who you become* through that process that matters more than actually reaching any one goal."

Hmmm. I gave the idea a minute to sink in. Obviously, Dan and I had discussed it before, but it now seemed to take on a deeper meaning. I thought, *What if I don't lower my goal? Even though selling $20,000 in ten days seems impossible, what if I stay committed and give it everything I have, regardless of my results? Would that help me become the type of person I need to be to achieve all of my future goals?* If I committed to selling $20,000 and giving it everything I had, regardless of the result, and the biggest payoff wasn't the goal itself but who I became in the process of trying to achieve it, I really couldn't fail. *Right? Right!* I decided to go for $20,000 in ten days.

I sat up in bed and turned on my bedside lamp. My brain was racing with ideas. I had to figure out how I was going to make this nearly impossible goal happen.

So at midnight and in my bed, I reverse engineered the push period that I was about to enter. I imagined that it was ten days into the future, and I asked myself, *If I had already sold $20,000, what would I have had to do between now and then?*

Because it was such a short time period, I knew that my fear of failure would be heightened. I asked myself, *How can I combat that fear?* The simplest answer was that I would have to believe that I could reach my goal, and I would have to maintain that belief until I did. Doing so would require telling myself over and over that I could reach my goal, especially when I had a bad day or my results weren't going well.

That initial belief evolved into Unwavering Faith.

Then I thought about how, when my results weren't going well, my drive to keep pushing forward would naturally diminish, because I would begin to doubt whether reaching the goal was possible. The way to combat that inertia would be to commit to giving it everything I had until the last possible moment, no matter what my results were along the way. I would have to maintain a high level of effort throughout.

That commitment became Extraordinary Effort.

Right then, I made two decisions that I knew I would have to maintain throughout the push period.

**DECISION 1:** I will establish and maintain Unwavering Faith that I can reach my goal of selling $20,000 during the push period, no matter what . . . there is no other option.

**DECISION 2:** I will put forth Extraordinary Effort every single day until the last possible moment, regardless of my results along the way.

I grabbed the notebook off my bedside table and wrote down both decisions to solidify my commitment. Then I combined them into a single sentence, a mantra that I could easily remember and recite to myself every day, which would remind me of my two decisions: *I am committed to maintaining Unwavering Faith that I will sell $20,000 for push, and putting forth Extraordinary Effort until I do, no matter what . . . there is no other option.*

I was still scared. And to be honest (and this is important to understand when you use the Miracle Equation yourself), I didn't actually believe I was going to sell $20,000 in the next ten days. Sure, I believed it was possible but definitely not *probable*. Our biggest goals usually aren't, which is part of what makes them miracles. Still, I was fully committed to giving it everything I had.

The math was simple. If I wanted to sell $20,000 in ten days, I needed to average $2,000 per day. That meant that in the first seven days, I would need to be over $14,000 in sales. Had I ever sold $2,000 in a day before? Sure. And I always celebrated, because a $2,000 day was both a great day and a pretty rare day. I considered a $2,000 day to be somewhat lucky. So to do that *every single day for 10 days in a row* would be quite the feat.

When I started the push period, luck was nowhere to be found. The first week was a roller coaster that ended in my finishing at only 50 percent of where I needed to be, to be on track for my goal. At only $7,000 in sales, and with just three days left to go, that was the position I'd feared I would be in. But I wasn't going to lower my goal. I had made a commitment to myself that I would give it everything I had until the last possible moment, no matter what. With only three days left, I set out to my first appointment of the day. While driving, I repeated my mantra: *I am committed to maintaining Unwavering Faith that I will sell $20,000 for push, and putting forth Extraordinary Effort* *until I do, no matter what . . . there is no other option.* Interestingly, the more I said it, the more I believed it.

Six Cutco presentations later, I finished the day with more than $3,000 in sales! That meant I was now over $10,000 for the push period. That day provided a much-needed boost, and I felt reenergized. I pulled my black Nissan Xterra over and took out my referral notebook to make calls. It was 7:00 p.m., prime phoning time. I pushed aside my concern about how I was going to sell $10,000 in the next two days and instead focused on making phone calls.

The next two days played out very similarly; I sold $3,238 on Tuesday and $4,194 on Wednesday, which put me at $17,024 for the push period. I was feeling inspired, but because our team was scheduled to meet the next morning at 7:00 a.m. to carpool to the conference in San Francisco, I was also out of time.

Or was I?

Not ready to give up short of my goal, I called Frank and asked him to let me skip the car pool so I could squeeze in a couple more appointments before the conference. Inspired by my commitment, he agreed.

I immediately pulled out my referral notebook and began making calls. Forty minutes later, I had my two appointments scheduled for the following morning. Although selling the remaining $3,000 during just two appointments certainly wasn't likely and in many people's perception not so realistic, it was definitely possible. As a bonus, I would have my good friend and colleague Adam Curchack with me. He had called me that evening to let me know he was going to be in town and asked if he could tag along on my appointments the next day.

The next morning, Adam met up with me, and we drove together to my first appointment. I was a ball of nervous energy! Could this actually happen? Cruising down the freeway, I rolled down my car window. Ignoring the fact that Adam was riding shotgun, I repeatedly shouted my mantra: "I am committed to maintaining  Unwavering Faith that I will sell $20,000 for push, and putting forth Extraordinary Effort until I do, no matter what . . . there is no other option! I am committed to maintaining  Unwavering Faith that I will sell $20,000 for push, and putting forth Extraordinary Effort until I do, no matter what . . . there is no other option!" The more I said it, the more I believed it. Adam cracked up laughing. He found my emphatic mantra yelling pretty amusing.

I pulled into Mrs. Hammerling's driveway at 7:58 a.m., then reached behind me and grabbed my navy blue Cutco brief bag filled with more than a dozen razor-sharp kitchen knives from the backseat, before Adam and I headed for her front door.

*Knock, knock.*

This was it. My palms were sweating. My heart was racing. I took a deep breath, looked at Adam, and recited my mantra in my head one last time: *I am committed to maintaining  Unwavering Faith that I will sell $20,000 for push, and putting forth Extraordinary Effort until I do, no matter what . . . there is no other option.*

No one answered, so I rang the bell. I glanced around the driveway and along the front of the house, not sure what I was expecting to see. Maybe Mrs. Hammerling was hiding in the bushes? I rang the bell again. Still no answer. I went back to my car for my cell phone and called Mrs. H. on her home phone, which was the only number I had for her. No answer. I called again . . . still no answer.

I was in disbelief. *This can't be happening!*

I waited around for half an hour. I called the house a few more times. Nothing. It was what we reps call a "no-show," and it couldn't have come at a worse time. I took a deep breath, and then Adam and I jumped back into my car and headed to my last appointment—my last chance to reach my goal. We arrived an hour early and parked down the street.

That hour wasn't good for me. It gave me too much time to think. Fear crept back in. I started to doubt myself. *How can this be happening?* I had given everything I had. I had maintained Unwavering Faith. I had put forth Extraordinary Effort. And now everything was riding on the next appointment. My last appointment. My stomach was in knots. Finally I knocked on Mrs. Carol Jones's door, silently repeating my miracle mantra: *I am committed to maintaining Unwavering Faith that I will sell $20,000 for push, and putting forth Extraordinary Effort until I do, no matter what . . . there is no other option!*

Thirty seconds later, the door opened. *Thank God.* I was now face-to-face with a forty-something-year-old blond woman.

"May I help you?" The woman's Swedish accent caught me off guard. This wasn't the woman I had spoken to on the phone.

"Are you Carol?" I asked.

Nope. She definitely wasn't Carol. Turned out she was Carol's sister-in-law, visiting from Sweden to attend her brother's fiftieth birthday party, which was a few days away. A quick phone call from the Swedish sister-in-law to Carol confirmed that Carol was across town and had completely forgotten about our appointment. She wasn't going to make it back in time. "Is there anything I can help you with?" the sister-in-law asked.

I thought for a second. *The Swedish sister-in-law on vacation for her brother's fiftieth birthday party isn't going to buy knives, right? Especially not $3,000 worth of knives.* "Thank you for asking, but I don't think so."

Adam cleared his throat and leaned over to me. "Hal," he said, "I drove all the way out here to watch you do a presentation. If this nice woman is willing to let you do the presentation, I'd still love to see it."

I looked at Adam as chills ran through my body. It was as if time stood still. The last possible moment hadn't arrived yet, and this nice woman was offering to help. Maybe, on some level, Adam had come along today to remind me of that?

"Actually, on second thought," I said to the woman, "there is something you can do to help. I was supposed to do a presentation for Carol to show her some high-quality kitchen cutlery, and this is my last appointment for the week. I would really appreciate if I could do my presentation for you, so I don't fall short with my appointments. Any chance you'd be up for that?"

Surprisingly, the Swedish sister-in-law was game. "Sure, come on inside!"

Adam smiled at me as we walked through the front door. I silently thanked him in my head. And as my last act of Extraordinary Effort, I proceeded to give the best, most enthusiastic Cutco presentation of my life.

Sixty minutes later, as I concluded my presentation and prepared to ask the sister-in-law if there was any chance she might want to purchase a set of Cutco, she said something that was hard to believe: "Hal, your timing is so interesting. My husband and I were just about to invest in a high-quality set of kitchen knives last week, back home in Sweden, but we both agreed that we should wait until after our trip here, to America. And on top of that, our entire family has been trying to find the perfect gift for my brother's fiftieth birthday, but we haven't found one yet. And he absolutely *loves* to cook, so this would be perfect!"

*What are the odds?* I thought to myself in disbelief. I smiled at her and nodded in anticipation.

"You know what, let's do it. I'll take two of your Ultimate Sets: one for my husband and me and one to give my brother for his birthday."

I had to keep myself from jumping out of my chair and hugging her. That sale put me over $3,000 for the day and exceeded my $20,000 goal!

As we drove away from that appointment, a conviction was born in me. I was beginning to understand that if I wanted an extraordinary life, these were the two decisions that would create it. Unwavering Faith, combined with Extraordinary Effort, was the formula to consistently produce extraordinary results. Tangible, measurable results that were so significant, and so unexpected, that they felt like miracles.

## TESTING THE EQUATION AND TEACHING IT TO OTHERS

The next push period became an experiment. I applied the same strategy. I created the possibility of selling $20,000 again, for what would be a record-setting fourth time. I committed to maintaining Unwavering Faith and putting forth Extraordinary Effort until the last possible moment, regardless of my results. However, this time it was with a curiosity as to whether the formula, which I had begun referring to in my journal as the "Miracle Equation," would work again.

It did. I finished the next push period at $23,701. Although I didn't fully understand it at the time, I was developing the qualities and the characteristics of a Miracle Maven, which would enable me to achieve any goal I set.

*Okay, but maybe it's just me. Maybe I'm just getting lucky*, I thought. I wanted to know for sure if the equation was real, so I began teaching it to my colleagues, fellow Cutco reps who had hired me to coach them. Geri Azinger, whose story you are about to read, was the first Cutco rep to whom I taught the Miracle Equation. As you'll see, Geri's story played out very similarly—almost identically, really—to my own.

## THE MIRACLE EQUATION IN ACTION

Back in the summer of 2005, Geri came to me because although she had consistently sold more than almost any other rep on a week-in, week-out basis, she had never been a big seller overall. Her largest push period had been just over $12,000, and she came to me asking if I could help her reach the next level, $15,000. I said, "No, but I'll help you sell $20,000, Geri, because I believe you can." And I told her about the Miracle Equation.

Geri's response was "I don't know. I've never done anything even close to that before. But I guess if the Miracle Equation works for you, Hal, I don't see why it won't work for me."

Much as my push period had started out, her first five sales demonstrations resulted in a whopping $1,000, not exactly the start she had been expecting. She made the decision to keep her faith in herself, and with renewed motivation, she set out for her second day. She went on to sell a few of the larger sets and ended the day with well over $3,000 in sales. The rest of the week continued on a sales roller coaster. By the beginning of the second week of the push, she was only at $8,500. She was scared, but she continued with her process, setting appointments and doing demos.

Fast-forward to the second Friday of the push. She was sitting at about $15,000 in sales. She needed a $5,000 weekend if she was going to get close to what she had originally set out to do. That night, she made fifty calls (more than she had ever done on a Friday night) and set seven demos for that weekend. Then she called me.

"Hal, I'm at $15,000! I'm still $5,000 away from my goal, and I'm definitely nervous, but I'm one hundred percent committed to implementing the Miracle Equation until the last possible moment. It's strange, but I actually believe it's going to happen! Or I should say, I have Unwavering Faith that I'm going to hit my goal, because there is no other option!"

That Saturday afternoon, she saw a very sweet couple who bought the largest set we sold at the time, the Ultimate Set, which was the same set I had sold to create my miracle. Not only did that couple give Geri a whole slew of referrals, but they took her next door and personally introduced her to their neighbor, who bought another Ultimate Set!

It was only 3:00 p.m., and she was already over $2,500 for the day. After a quick bite to eat, she hurried to her next demo. Bam! Another $1,000 sale. Back in her car, she connected with a potential customer she had been having a hard time getting ahold of. He told her that the only time he could do the appointment was after he got off work—at midnight. Reluctantly, she agreed. And it was a good thing she did. That demo, which she finished at two in the morning, pushed her over her sales goal.

But there was still time left in the competition, so she kept up her faith and effort and kept on selling. She finished that push period over $23,000, which was nearly double her previous best. The dream she'd once had had now become a reality. The Miracle Equation had proven itself to be true: Extraordinary Effort + Unwavering Faith = Miracles.

After Geri's experience, I continued to teach the Miracle Equation to dozens of my colleagues, and nearly every single person I taught it to created his or her own push-period miracle in excess of $20,000. Those results were unheard of.

My confidence in the validity of the formula grew. Rep after rep successfully broke through their self-imposed limiting mindset and produced tangible results beyond what they had once believed to be possible. To be clear, there was nothing else I was teaching them. There were no new sales techniques and no strategies to follow up with past customers. I told each of them my story of applying the Miracle Equation—the same story I just told you—and expanded on the principles of Unwavering Faith and Extraordinary Effort, as we're going to do throughout this book. And they applied it. That's it.

Then the Miracle Equation was proven to go even farther.

Robert Arauco, a relatively new sales rep who was putting himself through college, contacted me to help him reach his first $10,000 push period. Similar to what I told Geri, I told him that I believed he could double his goal and sell $20,000 by using the Miracle Equation, because I had seen it work for so many other people. Once I taught him the equation, he thought for a moment and then challenged my own paradigm. He asked, "Hal, do you think I could use the Miracle Equation to sell $30,000 in two weeks?" Personally, I had never reached that milestone, but I told him that I didn't believe there were any limits to the size of the miracle he could create. Robert went on to sell over $31,000 in two weeks, with more than $20,000 coming during the second week. By giving it everything he had until the last possible moment, he sold over $6,000 *in the last hour.*

The repeated success of the Miracle Equation proved that it wasn't a fluke and it wasn't luck. Rather, it was a proven, reliable, and repeatable strategy that, when understood and implemented correctly, would enable anyone to immediately begin accessing his or her full potential and creating results beyond what they ever had before.

## TESTING THE MIRACLE EQUATION BEYOND SALES REPS

You might be wondering *How does this apply to me?* I understand, because I wondered that myself: *Would the Miracle Equation work outside the sales world?* In fact, that is why it took me nearly twenty years to write this book. In addition to studying countless famous achievers to confirm the universal validity of the equation, I taught it to as many people as I could, who then used it to create all different kinds of miracles. I needed evidence that the Miracle Equation would work for any person, in any situation.

In short, it does.

Here's a short list of some of the people who have used the Miracle Equation successfully and shared their stories with me. Using the Miracle Equation:

Angela May was a single mom making $12,000 annually at Starbucks as a barista. That is, until she decided to start her own business. Within one year she made her first six figures and has gone on to grow her income to seven figures for the past three consecutive years.

Tim Nikolaev came over from Russia at age sixteen, learned the Miracle Equation at age seventeen (while working for Cutco), and used it to build the life of his dreams. Now in his early thirties, he is financially free and essentially retired (meaning his passive income from real estate exceeds his expenses and he works only if and when he wants). According to Tim, the most valuable lesson he learned was that you often can't predict how your path to a seemingly unreachable goal will play out, but by giving it everything you have until the last possible moment, regardless of your results along the way, you inevitably reach your goal—or something even better.

Shelley Boyes had a dream to establish a home for young women struggling with life-controlling issues such as eating disorders, drug and alcohol dependency, and the effects of abuse, anxiety, and depression, but she had no idea how to do so. The Miracle Equation revolutionized her thinking and made her believe that she could do whatever she believed was possible. Choose Life Ministry's Homestead for Hope is scheduled to open in September of this year.

Brandon LaBella had a dream to complete the 2017 New York City Marathon. Three days prior to the race, he tore the medial collateral ligament, on the inner side of his knee, and was confined to crutches. Instead of dropping out of the race, he looked up the fastest time on crutches completed at previous New York City Marathons and decided he was going to beat that time. Through the combined powers of Unwavering Faith and Extraordinary Effort, he decided that no matter what, he was going to finish the race. He went on to power through and beat the fastest time, setting a world record!

Carey Smolensky started a DJ company at the age of fourteen. While in dental school, he decided to leave and follow his passions, fueled by his Unwavering Faith and Extraordinary Effort to break the traditional mold and pursue a future in event production and entertainment. Now forty years later, his family of companies produces events globally, he has entertained over one million people, and he has grown his business to a level that grosses millions of dollars in revenue annually. Carey continues to use the Miracle Equation as he pursues his passions by writing a book about passion and successfully launching his own homegrown annual conference, the Passion Summit.

During 2016, Angel Morales traveled the world by himself for eleven months. He went to twenty-six countries on five different continents. He spent two years saving, researching, and preparing in order to accomplish his dream. When he told people he was going to quit his job and travel the world, no one believed him. But with his Unwavering Faith he bought the round-the-world ticket that made his dream a reality.

Alea Backus went from being a depressed, suicidal teenager who played video games all day to an aerial arts performer and teacher who inspires people of all ages to achieve their dreams and be resilient. As she continues to use the Miracle Equation, she's been able to triple her income in the last twelve months.

In twenty-four months, Ken Wimberly dropped more than thirty pounds, paid off $352,000 of debt, and scaled his brokerage business from $20 million to $70 million in annual sales.

Vencent Valenti married his dream woman, bought his dream home, wrote a children's book, and started two companies (and sold one).

Jessie Walters went from being bedridden with anxiety to being a successful real estate broker and a speaker at her church.

Mike Eaton lost ninety pounds and fulfilled his dream of being a stand-up comedian.

Theresa Laurico, the producer of The Miracle Morning movie, was hit by a bus and her body was devastated in the midst of our making the film (at the same time that I was undergoing cancer treatment). We leaned on each other and used the Miracle Equation simultaneously to fully recover.

When I was collecting these stories, I actually attempted to play devil's advocate and see if I could find people who did not utilize Unwavering Faith and Extraordinary Effort to achieve their goals, but I failed to find a single person.

I'll be sharing more stories throughout this book of individuals around the world, from world-famous Miracle Mavens to people whose names you probably don't know, who have successfully created tangible, measurable miracles using the equation. Each story serves as evidence of what's possible for *you*. The beauty of the equation is that it works for any goal, big or small, and for anyone who makes and *maintains* the two decisions.

## YOUR OWN MIRACLE EQUATION JOURNEY

The remainder of this book will serve as your bridge, of sorts, to the life you want—not by simply wishing for it but by understanding how to move from wanting it to creating it. I will walk you through this process—and it is a process—so that producing tangible, measurable miracles ultimately becomes your norm. When you choose to embody the two decisions, you become a Miracle Maven, and you'll think and live differently from the way you have in the past, which will push you toward different results in your present and future.

The first step in embodying this new Miracle Maven identity is to identify and overcome the inherent human conflict that we all have but usually aren't aware of. In the next chapter, we'll lay out this conflict, see how it might be manifesting in your life, and then work on getting out from under it so you can achieve the results you want.

# 3

# THE INHERENT HUMAN CONFLICT

Moving from Limited to Limitless

The world we live in—the life we perceive—is a perfect reflection, a mirror image, of our internal reality.

—PATRICK CONNOR

There's a chance that you, like so many people, have forgotten a really basic fact about yourself: *You. Are. Limitless.*

Human beings are designed for greatness, and proof of that fact abounds. Every day, previously held limitations are shattered as another one of us taps into our shared limitless potential and sets new standards for what we are *all* capable of achieving. Anything that another person has done is evidence of what's possible for you. Everything you want for your life is available to you right now, just waiting for you to make the decision and go after what you want.

If you think back to your childhood, you might be able to remember feeling this about yourself. Becoming a famous ballerina or baseball player seemed totally plausible and within your reach. You never considered that you might not achieve what your mind's eye was showing you. *Everything was possible.* Your future was limitless. Some of us have lost this awareness completely. Others can retrieve this perspective with enough prompting or reminiscing about "what could have been." Even then, though, this feeling seems distant and no longer relevant to the life they are living today. A life with a pile of bills on the counter, a job that doesn't fulfill them, and a few extra pounds they just can't get rid of. But not remembering this information does not make it not true, nor does it make it any less relevant.

So how did we forget this important fact?

Through no fault of our own, we've been unknowingly sabotaging ourselves, and it only gets worse as we get older. I know, that's not very encouraging, but it's true. We're up against some harsh obstacles in life, both inside our own heads and in the world around us. And these obstacles can be a bit sneaky. Oftentimes, we don't even know that they exist.

To start, we have these innate tendencies that are hardwired into our brain and constantly knock us off our path to greatness. Our inborn human nature leads us to take the easy road, doubt ourselves, and give up when things get difficult. The easy path is usually more comfortable in the short term, and our brains translate that comfort into *this must be what I should be doing.*

Then, as we're growing up and ripe to absorb messages (both spoken and unspoken) from those around us, we are taught to follow the rules, fit in, and play along. We even allow the irrational limiting beliefs of others to influence our own and stifle our ideas of what's possible for us. Our loved ones offer a pat on the back and the requisite "You gave it a good shot" but never hold us accountable for stretching into our full potential, probably because they're not fulfilling their own. We support each other right into the depths of mediocrity.

After a while, we join the conformists and eventually buy into the whole "why I can't be amazing" song and dance. We accumulate an arsenal of self-sabotaging limitations that, for the most part, we don't even realize we have. We put forth *just enough* effort to get by. We run through our days on autopilot, often with no clear goal or intention. We allow others to impose limits on us. Ultimately, we settle for less than we truly want and are capable of. In part, both our brains and our well-meaning friends and family members hold our life of miracles hostage.

Sheesh. How's a guy or gal supposed to create an extraordinary life with all these hurdles constantly thrust upon him or her?

Good question. The answer lies in understanding the inherent human conflict we all face: **Deep down inside, we know that we are limitless. But our own brains and the world around us confine us so we remain smaller than we should be.** This conflict leads to unhappiness, anxiety, and the constant feeling that there is something else—something more—out in this world for us. We know it, but we don't know what to do about it.

Until now.

To create the most extraordinary life you can imagine—the one you want, deserve, and are destined for—you must overcome this inner conflict and take the path that leads to greatness, which won't necessarily be the easiest path, the option that feels more comfortable or even safest. When you feel yourself haggling in your head over a decision that comes down to your being limited (based on your past) or limitless (based on your potential), choose limitless. Period.

It's not easy. I never said it would be. But it is possible, and specifically, it is possible for *you*. If you are willing to read to the end of this chapter, you're going to get a lot of new insights into what is standing between you and the miraculous life that you deserve to live. And you're going to realize, *Wow, I can totally do this.*

So let's get started.

## THE WAR YOU WAGE WITH YOURSELF

Let's gain some perspective. Wherever you are in your life right now, whether you're at the top of your game or enduring circumstances that are unpleasant, painful, or somewhere in between, consider this: *You are exactly where you're supposed to be (and who you're supposed to be) to learn what you need to learn so you can become the person you need to be who is capable of creating everything you've ever wanted.* Whew. That's a mouthful, but I believe every word of it. I hope you do, too. Every experience you've had up until this point in your life, including those that have been the most difficult, is an asset when you choose to learn from it.

Here's the rub (and where you need to step in): It may or may not be your fault if you're not living the life you want, but it *is* your responsibility to make the changes necessary to go to the next level. No one is going to do it for you. Choosing to live your life at Level 10 is up to you. And the first step to getting there is to overcome this internal conflict.

The choice to live either a limited or a limitless life shows up in all sorts of ways: Should I leave my job and start my own business? Should I leave this relationship when I don't know if I'll find someone else? Do I really have to stop eating the foods I enjoy if I want to drop ten pounds? Each of these decisions impacts a different area of your life. Still, they all boil down to being *limited—by your past, your fears, your failures, or other people—versus limitless.* Think about a decision that is on your mind right now. Can you filter it through this lens? Does it look any different when you do so?

When I was writing *The Miracle Morning*, I constantly battled fear and self-doubt that tempted me to give up and stop writing. Though I believed so much in the concept and had seen the results firsthand, my inner voice kept standing in my way: *Who am I to convince people that they should wake up early? How can I possibly compel anyone to overcome the deeply ingrained limiting belief of "I am not a morning person" that they've likely believed (and their behavior has reinforced) for their entire lives?* Thankfully, I didn't allow my internal conflict to have the final say in what I did. I refused to let my fears dictate my actions.

Though we could surely identify hundreds, maybe thousands, of ways this conflict shows up in our lives, there are four internal conflicts that tend to show up most often and that we must overcome. First, we have a brain that registers new opportunities as *dangerous.* We also reject the notion that we are deserving of all that we want and instead settle for mediocre effort and results in one, several, or all areas of our lives. We lose sight of our innate gifts and fail to see all that we can accomplish. Finally, we allow the world to influence our thinking and even define us, which usually leads us to believe that we are less capable than we actually are. Standing against all of these limitations is the belief that inside of you, there is potential left untapped. So our internal angst persists.

Alone, each of these conflicts is enough to put a real dent in your grand plans for life. Together, though, they make it nearly impossible to navigate your way to what you really want. Let's go deeper and explore each conflict, so we can understand where it comes from and what the results will be if you don't overcome it. Toward the end of the chapter, we will discuss how to overcome each of these conflicts so you can start moving toward creating the life you've been waiting for.

## THE IRRATIONAL FEAR OF OPPORTUNITY VERSUS MAINTAINING THE STATUS QUO

Most of us fall into cycles of getting all excited about a new goal and then abruptly stopping, either when things get tough or even before we begin. Why is this?

It all starts with the human brain. The human brain is pretty incredible. It's the central command center of our bodies. It keeps our lungs breathing, our heart pumping, and our body moving. It even enables us to determine how good or bad our life is by focusing on the aspects of our lives that make us feel good or those that cause us to feel bad. All that we do or don't do begins with our brain. But even though our brain enables us to experience life, it also gets in the way of our creating the life we want.

Though we're all born with limitless potential, we're also born with a brain that operates under many of its primitive, prehistoric reflexes. We are hardwired to scan our environments for danger because back in the caveman days, not spotting a fast-moving lion meant a painful death. Eating the wrong greens could be toxic. We could encounter life-and-death situations multiple times a week. We were just trying to get through another day, literally. Luckily, most of us don't run into these types of experiences often—or ever. But our brain doesn't know that. It's still paranoid, always scanning for potential threats, in a constant attempt to keep us safe.

Instead of fearing death, though, our brains are on high alert for anything that could take us out of our comfort zone. The fear of death has been replaced by the fear of failure and discomfort, both emotional and physical. Staying safe is no longer only about avoiding predators; now we avoid opportunities, too. For the most part, we fear the unknown. When a new opportunity pops up that would give us the chance to develop ourselves further into the person we would like to be, our brain sounds the panic alarm. We immediately run through everything that could go wrong: *I could fail, I could be embarrassed, I could be disappointed.* All of this stress makes it hard to make intelligent decisions and disrupts our emotional well-being. Sometimes it can feel as though our emotions control us, rather than the other way around.

Our external circumstances begin to dictate our internal state. We become reactive and lose the space in which we can calmly think through how to respond optimally in any given situation. When our emotions take control, it is nearly impossible to stay focused on our goals, as any minor setback feels insurmountable. So we continuously crawl back into the cave that is our comfort zone. Although it's dark in there, it feels safe.

All of our energy and mental focus is directed toward trying to turn off that stress response (which, by the way, makes it worse), and we then interpret a great opportunity as being too hard, too dangerous, and just too much to attempt. Any opportunity that pulls us away from what we have come to understand as our norm is perceived as something to be avoided.

Miracle Mavens have figured out something that the rest of us haven't: how to bypass this stress response. Or, more accurately stated, how to turn it off when it's harmful or holding them back. They have trained their brain to understand the difference between an uncomfortable situation and one that is truly life or death. They consistently choose to replace the fear of what could go wrong by consciously choosing to focus on and maintain the faith that things will likely go right. They invest time on exploring and pursuing the possibilities that will make them happy and fulfilled, even though they know that the possibility of failure always exists (although as you'll learn in chapter 5, "A New Paradigm of Possibility," it actually doesn't). Rather than dwelling on their fears and past failures, Miracle Mavens understand how crucial it is to both have faith in themselves and actively figure out which steps they must take to turn their most meaningful goals into reality. By actually taking control of their brain, they've taken control of their lives.

Most of us have not. From high school students yet to enter the workforce all the way up to Fortune 500 CEOs, we all struggle with irrational fears and an overactive stress response. We need to consider how our irrational fears suck the air from our dreams and the lives that we could be living. Instead of fearing and avoiding opportunities, we need to take a deep breath—and then run toward them. We need to be willing to fail, learn from our mistakes, and try again. We need to replace our fear with faith (lots more on that to come). Really, there is no other way to overcome this conflict and achieve success.

## MISDIRECTED ENTITLEMENT VERSUS ENLIGHTENED ENTITLEMENT

However you define Level 10 success, I'm sure that if you are reading this book, you would like to have more of it. But what level of success do you believe that you deserve?

Unfortunately, most of us don't truly believe or genuinely feel that we deserve much more than we have or have seen those close to us have. Whatever levels of success, happiness, and fulfillment we are accustomed to become our norm and the standard for what we expect in our future. In that way, we keep perpetuating our past with no plans to live larger moving forward. So many of us never even get out of the gate because we don't really believe that we deserve what's at the end of the road. In order to become a Miracle Maven, you're going to have to believe not only that your biggest goals and dreams are possible, probable, and inevitable . . . but that you *deserve* to achieve them. Without that last piece, you'll never get to the goal because you don't really believe you deserve to be there. You'll always find an excuse to back away from your greatness. But when you believe that you're entitled to success, you will fight for it.

Now, I know that using the word *entitled* can make some folks feel icky. The word *entitlement* is often associated with individuals who believe they deserve special privileges or resources, though they've done nothing to earn them. A sense of entitlement is often linked with narcissism or arrogance, and a person with an entitlement complex is similar to a child who has never learned that he or she is not the center of the universe. This describes a sense of deservedness regardless of whether or not any effort has been put forth. This is what most people think of as entitlement. But there are two other forms of entitlement, both of which you need to be aware of. One you should move toward. The other you should avoid.

*Enlightened Entitlement*, which is what we should all strive for, is characterized by the fundamental belief that each of us is just as deserving, worthy, and capable of creating and having anything we want for our lives (that is, anything we're willing to put in the effort to achieve) as any other person on Earth. Nearly every great accomplishment begins with an individual believing that he or she is capable of putting forth the effort to accomplish it *and* that he or she deserves the subsequent success. This kind of entitlement is healthy and a prerequisite to creating tangible, measurable miracles. It reinforces our belief in our own potential and our recognition of that potential. To be clear, this is hard for many people, myself included. We turn away from recognition of our efforts. We blush when someone praises or thanks us for a job well done. Sometimes we even reject the reward outright; "It really wasn't a big deal," we say, even when it was. Receiving praise feels uncomfortable. Think about how much harder it is to pursue a goal when you don't really feel that you deserve it. It's virtually impossible to put in the effort necessary to create miraculous results when you don't feel entitled to them.

In many cases, Enlightened Entitlement is what you'll use to ignite your Unwavering Faith. You'll find it's often easier to believe that you deserve the end result than believing that you can accomplish it. But this is not the case for everyone or for every miracle. Speaking for myself, I know that digging up this deserving feeling doesn't always come so easily. I see other people struggling or those less fortunate and think, *Why do I deserve to be any happier or more successful than they are?* Keep in mind that sometimes you need to gain a little traction with your Extraordinary Effort before you can experience Enlightened Entitlement. As you begin to put forth consistent effort, and the more effort you put forth, the more deserving you will naturally feel. The order is less important than the fact that you must own that you deserve anything you want and are willing to put in the effort for, in order for the Miracle Equation to work. Miracle Mavens own their contribution and feel deserving of the rewards of their efforts.

On the other end of the spectrum, we have *Misdirected Entitlement*, which is really laziness masquerading as a feeling of deservedness. We tell ourselves, "Oh, I deserve this cookie. I've been pretty good about my eating." Or "I deserve to buy this thing I don't really need. I've been pretty good about my spending." Or "I deserve to miss the gym. I've been pretty good about working out." Do any of these sound familiar to you? We all do this from time to time, but it is harmful.

This kind of behavior reinforces mediocrity; we treat ourselves for being "pretty good." But "pretty good" isn't great and certainly doesn't get us any closer to miraculous results. It simply allows you to give yourself a pat on the back for subpar performance. It gives you permission to be lazy. Just as overworking yourself to the point of exhaustion and burnout is unhealthy, doing less than you know you should be doing is detrimental to reaching your goals.

Accepting mediocre effort from yourself holds you back from achieving Level 10 success, and your level of effort that is needed is relative to whatever it is that you're attempting to accomplish. A person who is training for a marathon might need to run five days a week, while someone who is trying to get healthier may need to walk for only thirty minutes a few times a week. And only you know the truth about how much effort you're putting forth when no one else is watching. Your definition of Level 10 success is also unique to you and whatever you are trying to accomplish. The point is to align your actions and the amount of effort needed with your goal so that you feel deserving of it and avoid falling into the trap of being lazy.

Let's be honest: being lazy feels nice. Who doesn't enjoy watching television, lying around the house, with no responsibilities, no concerns, and no guilt. *But* (and this is a big *but*) in order to be lazy with no guilt, you have to accomplish something first to award yourself *earned* laziness. I have a rule to spend time with my kids, do something that adds value to my wife's life, and complete all of my work-related tasks before I get to enjoy "guilt-free" laziness. If you're going to binge on Netflix, there's no judgment here; just make sure you do it *after* you've accomplished your most important priorities for the day.

One major problem with laziness when it's not preceded by doing anything to earn it is that it prevents you from feeling entitled to greater success. When you don't put forth sustained effort, you don't really deserve what you're striving for, and you know it. This causes you not to believe in yourself, and not to believe that you deserve anything better than you have now. This is why Misdirected Entitlement is so dangerous.

Another roadblock that we throw up in front of ourselves, which is another manifestation of Misdirected Entitlement, is "staying busy." How many times have you told yourself that you can't take advantage of a new opportunity or find the time to work on your biggest dream because you were (drumroll . . .) *too busy*? Being too busy is essentially doing things that don't really matter, so we trick ourselves into thinking we're being productive. Responding to dozens of emails might make us feel as though we're being productive and, in turn, deserving, but deep down, we know it's a lie.

In Cal Newport's groundbreaking book *Deep Work: Rules for Focused Success in a Distracted World*, he explains that our ability to perform deep work, or to focus on one task that requires a lot of brainpower for an extended amount of time, is decreasing just as this very skill is becoming more of an asset. Those who can develop this skill will be rewarded for it. In the context of miracles, only those who can detach themselves from the distractions around them, move beyond spending time on inconsequential tasks, and instead focus their mental (and physical) energy on a single objective for an extended period of time are able to create tangible, measurable miracles. Staying busy by wasting time on lower-priority activities directly opposes this notion.

When we look at our to-do list, it's very natural to gravitate toward the lower-priority, lower-risk activities, which have the fewest significant consequences attached to them. These activities might include checking email, posting on social media, doing online research, any form of organizing, whether physical or digital, or even personal development if you're using it to justify procrastinating on other higher-priority tasks. By staying busy with low-priority activities, we keep ourselves distracted and safe from engaging in the activities that actually matter and that will move us in the direction of achieving our most significant goals and dreams. Doing high-priority activities can be scary, as they come with significant consequences that could be meaningful in our lives and that could force us to flex our "I deserve" muscle. Staying busy with low-priority activities is a behavior that keeps us from feeling we deserve the success we want.

## POTENTIAL DYSMORPHIA VERSUS ACTUALIZED POTENTIAL

You'll read a little later on about when I was diagnosed with a very rare and aggressive form of cancer at the age of thirty-seven. When I first began cancer treatment, my weight quickly dropped from 167 to 127 pounds. Thirty of those pounds were dropped in the first three weeks. At just over six feet tall, my cheekbones became more prominent, as did my ribs and hip bones. I also lost every hair on my body. The interesting thing was that when I looked in the mirror, I just saw the same old me, minus the hair. I didn't see a skinny cancer patient looking back at me; I saw the same person I had always been.

I knew intellectually that my body must look different. I mean, forty pounds is a lot of weight to lose, especially for someone who was already thin. In fact, roughly one-fourth of my body weight had disappeared in a matter of weeks. When I mentioned to my wife, Ursula, that I thought I still looked pretty much the same, the expression on her face told me that I did not. Not to mention that my well-meaning parents kept trying to feed me every chance they got. The messages I got from the outside world were quite different from my internal perceptions. In this case, my perception of myself was skewed.

I thought, *This must be how somebody with body dysmorphia— someone who suffers significant insecurities over a perceived or minor physical flaw—feels, but in reverse.* Such folks will exercise to exhaustion because they think they are fat, when the scale clearly shows they are at a healthy weight. They obsess over how to deflect attention away from their nose, which they've decided is too big for their face, even though no one else even notices. They cannot see their body in an accurate way. And neither could I.

Unfortunately, we do this with our own potential, too. We don't see what we are truly capable of. In fact, if you were to pause and listen to your thoughts for a moment, you would probably hear a lot of negative statements that most of us unconsciously repeat to ourselves: *I'm unworthy. I'm unlucky. I'm too busy. I'm lazy. I don't know where to start. He/she is better than I am. I've tried to improve this area of my life, but I never stick with it.* Negative statements such as these are the recording that we listen to on constant rotation in our heads. We hear them enough that we believe them to be true and then act accordingly.

We point to past failures and say, "Nope, I'm not going to try that again." We internalize slights that we've received about our abilities over the years. We look for evidence to support and even prove our limitations. After all that, we arrive at conclusions as to what we believe is realistic or likely to achieve based on our paradigm of our past and end up with the false belief that we are less capable than we actually are. There isn't a single person on the planet, including the most successful, who doesn't look back to his or her past and see failures. What's important is that you don't have to live that way; you can consciously choose to make decisions based on your limitless future.

In *The Miracle Morning*, I included a bonus chapter titled "The Email That Will Change Your Life." I told a story about the time I realized that I didn't have an accurate view of my strengths and weaknesses, so I sent an email to over twenty of the people who knew me well and asked for their honest feedback. This group included family, friends, colleagues, mentors, and even a couple of former girlfriends. The responses I received were both eye opening and motivating, and a little painful. It was like seeing myself in 3-D; I finally saw all of me, both how I viewed myself and how I appeared to a variety of people who knew me in various capacities. That exercise changed my life, because I embraced the feedback I received, wrote it down, and proceeded to make changes to my behavior, accordingly. This exercise has also changed the lives of many others who have tried it. If you think you might not be able to accurately see all of yourself (and you probably can't), this is definitely an exercise to consider.

All those who have ever gone from being average to being extraordinary began by first seeing themselves as better than they had ever been in the past. They were willing to see a vision for themselves based on their limitless capabilities and then begin living in alignment with that vision. It's rarely easy to do at first—few things are—as it can feel inauthentic. However, when you revisit that vision often (see: daily) over time, it comes to feel more and more true, because it is the real you. Eventually, over time, your new vision becomes your new identity and inevitably your new reality.

## THE WORLD DEFINES YOU VERSUS YOU DEFINE YOU

If you've ever stuffed yourself into an old pair of jeans that are too small, you know how uncomfortable it can be. The button digs into your abdomen. The fabric grips your legs. It may even be hard to walk normally. Not only is that not a good look, but it's uncomfortable.

The reality is that we do something similar with our lives. When we allow others to dictate who we should be, we end up pushing down our instincts to be a little different. To do things on our own terms. To fight for what we really want. We stuff ourselves into a mold that other people believe we should fit into. In the process, we come to feel as though we can't move as freely as we would like, confined or restricted or even controlled by the expectations of others, and that feels uncomfortable.

For the most part, we've been taught to think small, to stay within the lines, to fit in and follow the rules, *other people's rules.* These rules are designed to help us fit into society, but they work counter to our innate desire to achieve Level 10 success. Nowhere in my formal education was I taught how to think outside the box, explore my unique gifts, or discover which rules the world's most successful people played by, which would have given me a clear road map showing me the way to join them. Where was that curriculum?

The standard life track is to go to school, get a steady job, and work until you're sixty-five, when hopefully you'll have enough money for a mediocre retirement. We are conditioned to be responsible, docile, and average—to fit in. But all of this behavior is learned. It has nothing to do with the person that you are or, rather, can choose to be.

Eventually we learn to distrust our own instincts and become cynical toward ourselves. We see people who achieve extraordinary success as outliers. They are "different." Starting from childhood and over many years, we are conditioned by other people's beliefs about

## OVERCOMING LIMITATIONS IN ACTION

Recently, I was introduced to one of the most inspiring people I have ever met, twenty-two-year-old Nick Santonastasso. Nick was born with Hanhart syndrome, an extremely rare genetic condition that left him without legs, a right arm that is not fully formed, and a left arm with only one finger. In Nick's "My Life Story" YouTube video, which he posted in 2014, he explained that there are only twelve known cases of Hanhart syndrome. Nick was one of only four people still alive with the condition.

Incredibly, he never let these physical limitations get in the way of his interests or dreams. Nick skateboards, wake-surfs behind boats, was on his high school varsity wrestling team, has competed in fitness competitions, and is a fitness model. He has also appeared on CNN and Fox and become an online star with his hilarious YouTube videos. When Nick appeared on the *Today* show at twelve years of age, in response to a question about where he had gotten his feeling of being limitless, he said that he knew that anything was possible; he just wanted to try things that he thought would be fun and that he might like. He had no fear of failing because he knew that he could just get back up and try again.

Despite the great odds stacked against him, Nick has never faltered in who he is and what he wants, and he has created an extraordinary life for himself. He has refused to let the world's perceptions of him define him. He has always known exactly who he was and that he was destined for greatness, no matter what— there was no other option. In addition to being a bodybuilder and fitness model, Nick is now sharing his message of inspiration as a motivational speaker. In fact, I just booked him to deliver his keynote message at next year's Best Year Ever [Blueprint] live event.

what is possible for us. And although forcing ourselves into this mold might be the path of least resistance, it has landed us where we are now, looking for a way to scratch that "I know I'm capable of more" itch.

As Nick realized, deep within, we know that we are capable of more. And we want more. We want to live a meaningful life and make a difference in the world. Many of us can hear that inner voice telling us that we are capable of doing both. It might be a quiet voice and is often drowned out by fears and insecurities, but it's there. Maybe you've heard this voice inside yourself?

So how do you define yourself?

If you can't yet answer that question in any kind of meaningful way, don't worry. Many people can't. Instead we spout off a bunch of labels that have been given to us by others and take them as gospel. *I am a wife/husband, mother/father, lawyer/student, creative/analytical, homemaker/provider.* The labels can go on forever, but do they really capture you as the limitless being that you are?

As children, we were all labeled in some way. Whether it was a clinical diagnosis or just a nickname that our family gave us, the problem is that we often grew into the labels given to us as children. Some of us were *angels* (my sister). Others were *troublemakers* (me). Still others might have been *good athletes* or *artists.*

Those names and labels helped to shape our identity based on how those around us saw us. We quickly learned who we were based on other people's perceptions of us. Those labels also, to some degree, shaped our friendship circle, our activities, our likes and dislikes, and our ambitions for the future. Now, I'm not saying that silly childhood nicknames and medical diagnoses are inherently bad. Nicknames are often a term of affection (people haven't stopped calling me "Yo Pal Hal" ever since my mom gave me the nickname for my job as a radio DJ when I was fifteen). Medical diagnoses can guide us toward the help we need. The problem arises when we allow those names and labels to define us and limit us. Then those limits follow us into adulthood, where we continue to look to others to tell us who we are.

I'm especially aware of this with my children and try to safeguard them against labels that could define and confine them. My daughter, for example, thinks that she has ADHD, and I'm not even sure why. She's never been formally diagnosed and none of her teachers has given her that label. I guess it's possible that she has heard me talk about my own ADHD (I was formally diagnosed as an adult). Regardless of how she got it into her head, I don't want her to use this self-diagnosis as a way to limit what she believes she's capable of.

When we talk about it together, I describe ADHD as a character trait that some of us are fortunate to have. It enables us to be creative and to stumble on great ideas (since our minds are constantly bouncing from one idea to the next). I've also googled phrases such as "famous/successful people with ADHD" and shown her stories of people who never let the diagnosis limit them, and I've pointed out their accomplishments to her as evidence that it can be an advantage. I also explain to her that although we may have to work a little harder to stay focused, it's not that we "can't." My point for her is that no one but she herself will define what she can do. Some days she accepts my explanation more easily than others. As adults often do, she sometimes fights for her limitations.

## . . . AND THEN WE JUSTIFY OUR LIMITATIONS

We've all been hurt, let down, and disappointed. We've all experienced situations that we wish had gone one way but didn't. And, yes, all of those things sucked. But what sucks even more is when we allow such experiences to color our whole world. Our fear of being hurt again prevents us from taking risks and pursuing opportunities. It keeps us living small.

Even worse is when we allow the hurt to nudge us toward the self-destructive cycle of arguing for our limitations, meaning that we continuously reinforce the belief that we cannot do, be, or have something we want because of some sort of isolated experience. We give ourselves an "out" at every new opportunity, because we assume that we aren't qualified or capable, or that it probably won't work out, and then we scratch our head, wondering why the life of our dreams hasn't played out quite as we had hoped.

Have you ever heard someone justify their complaining by saying something like "I'm not negative; I'm just realistic"? This is a classic case of arguing for your own limitations. Really, it's not even logical. Consider this: How is it any more "realistic" to focus on and verbalize our limitations (which inevitably discourages us from taking meaningful steps to improve) than it is to focus on and verbalize our limitless capabilities (which gives us strength and reminds us that we have the ability to improve and accomplish anything)? Both are equally realistic, but which one you consistently focus on has a very different impact on both the quality of your current life, and your future.

Besides, no one really knows what is and isn't possible. We simply don't know what we don't know. Every day, things that were once considered impossible become possible and eventually the norm. Experts once believed that it wasn't possible for a man (or woman) to run a mile in under four minutes. As you know, that all changed in

1954 when the British runner Roger Bannister made the impossible possible when he ran a mile in just 3 minutes and 59.4 seconds. Forty-six days later, John Landy broke Bannister's record. Now high school students routinely surpass the four-minute mark.

Some of us remember the time before email, text messaging, and fax machines, when snail mail was the best mode of transferring letters and business documents from one person to another. I have trouble remembering how we drove to new locations (especially at night) before we had GPS. There was a time, not so long ago, when we didn't have cell phones seemingly attached to our palms. Today I have a talking robot in my house named Alexa that plays music for my family, sets reminders, looks up recipes, tells my kids stories, turns our lights on and off, buys things for me online, and does all sorts of other things. A few years ago, that was possible only in science fiction movies, and now it's our everyday reality. Had any of the people who discovered these advancements given in to their skeptic's "logic," our world would look very different than it does today.

When it comes to how the future unfolds and how the universe actually works, it's very likely that there is more that we do not yet understand than we do. So although a healthy level of skepticism about our limitless nature can be a good thing, a healthy level of optimism might be even better.

## THE WAY TO OVERCOME ALL THESE CONFLICTS

How can we escape this inner conflict and step into unlimited success in all areas of our life when there are so many hurdles before us? Many people spend years in therapy, countless dollars on personal coaches, and a lot of time banging their heads against the wall in the name of finding their happiness. Now, I'm not saying that therapy or personal coaching is not helpful. I am a firm believer in both. But

I also believe that people can get a lot of mileage out of living their life in alignment with the two simple but life-altering decisions we've begun exploring, which you're now very familiar with: Unwavering Faith and Extraordinary Effort. Remember the feedback loop that we discussed in chapter 1? Here is where it becomes critical.

When you take the leap into Enlightened Entitlement and *decide* that you deserve everything you want and are willing to put in the effort for, and then you actively believe in your limitless capabilities instead of buying into your self-imposed limitations, you build the energy and motivation needed to improve your life. The more you do this, the more authentic you realize it is—and, in turn, the more faith you have in yourself. You know that you are capable of anything because *you* dictate what you can and cannot do. Not your past. Not your parents. Not society. Only you. Making and maintaining these two decisions *over an extended period of time* is how you break free of your innate conflict between the desire to be limitless and your perceived limitations.

This feedback loop will automatically put you on the path to creating tangible, measurable miracles. I realize that this may seem a bit anticlimactic, there being only these two seemingly simple decisions that will supposedly pull you out of your lifelong internal conflict—the primary reason that persistent high levels of success have eluded you in the past—but this is really what it takes. Don't let your irrational fear of opportunity deter you from experiencing it for yourself.

Now that you understand the four fundamental manifestations of the inherent human conflict and how to overcome them, we can move into the next chapter, which will tell you exactly how to get yourself into the optimum emotional state for the Miracle Equation to work. Hint: You'll need to release every negative emotion that's ever held you back. But, as you're about to read, this will take only about five minutes. I promise.

# 4

# BECOMING EMOTIONALLY INVINCIBLE

How to Release Every Negative
Emotion That's Ever Held You Back

The pain that you create now is always
some form of nonacceptance,
some form of unconscious resistance
to what is. On the level of thought,
the resistance is some form of judgment.
On the emotional level,
it is some form of negativity.

—ECKHART TOLLE

Don't you just hate those hectic mornings when you're running late and soon after you pull your car out of your driveway, you discover that there's been a car accident on the freeway and traffic is at a standstill? You've got somewhere you need to be, and bumper-to-bumper traffic is the last thing you need this particular morning! Or worse, how about the person who may have also been running late but was the one involved in the accident? *Poor soul*, you think. *They've got it even worse than I do.* Of course, you take a millisecond to hope they're okay, but your attention quickly goes back to yourself and your endless supply of problems to worry about.

Or what about when you are counting on a big deal to close. You've been working on it for months. It's going to bring in a lot of money for your company and raise your company's reputation in your industry. Amazingly, all of the details have fallen into place along the way. Now you only have to get the signed agreement. But it doesn't arrive on the day that your contact had promised. When you reach out to check on the agreement, you get the dreaded email that the other side is backing out. *Nooo!!!!!* After you read the email for the third time, you close the door to your office and sulk over your lost deal—for the rest of the day.

How about when you buy two tickets to a concert and plan to go with your significant other. This is your favorite band, and you've both been looking forward to this evening for months. You make some dinner reservations for the two of you beforehand and even buy a new outfit for the special night. There is no one you'd rather share this experience with than your partner, and nothing is going to stop you from seeing the concert. But then, a week beforehand, your other half tells you that he or she has to go on a work trip instead. You spend the next several days complaining about your disappointment to anyone who will listen.

Life can really suck at times. There are so many aspects of life that are out of our control, and nobody likes feeling out of control. But there's a light at the end of the tunnel, because there is a proven approach that essentially eliminates all negative emotions in the span of five minutes or less. Let's back up for a moment and make the connection between feeling negative emotions and creating tangible, measurable miracles. As we've discussed, miracles are born out of possibility—the notion that anything is possible for you and that you deserve all of the success you're willing to put in the effort for. However, when your emotional state isn't optimal—whether you're experiencing stress, fear, worry, regret, resentment, or any other unpleasant emotion—you're not thinking about what's possible. You're not fine-tuning your plans or brainstorming creative solutions to your problems. You're not filled with energy. No, you're dwelling on your negative emotions. You're licking your wounds, so to speak. Meanwhile, the possibilities are passing you by because there's no space in your brain for anything more than those negative emotions.

Have you ever considered what the fundamental cause is of every negative emotion that you've ever felt? I'm talking about *every* negative emotion—anger, rage, frustration, sadness, sorrow, fear, disappointment, boredom, hate, annoyance, embarrassment, guilt, worry—you name it. If you were to give it some thought, you'd probably come up with a different cause for each time you felt a negative emotion. We always have something or someone to blame for the way that we feel. *I'm angry because of what he said. I'm upset because of what happened. I'm sad because of what (or whom) I lost. I'm stressed because I have too much on my plate. I'm worried because things might not work out the way I've planned.* We mistakenly assume that the causes of our emotional pain are the circumstances, situations, and people that don't meet our expectations. Nothing could be further from the truth.

Our emotional pain and those times we've felt bad have far less to do with what's going on *around* us and everything to do with what's going on *inside* us. After reading this chapter, you won't ever have to feel bad again. What you're about to learn defies both human nature and what we've been conditioned to believe causes our negative emotions, and it is the key that unlocks the door to emotional invincibility. Becoming emotionally invincible means that *you* will be in control of your emotions, and you don't ever have to feel emotional pain again, unless, of course, you want to (and as you'll soon find out, there are actually times when you'll probably want to).

## TAKING RESPONSIBILITY FOR OUR NEGATIVE EMOTIONS

I know that this is going to sound harsh, but I just have to get it out there: *Every painful emotion that you have ever felt, are feeling now, and will ever feel in the future was, is, and will be self-created by you and is completely optional.* I'm talking about *every* painful or even unpleasant emotion that causes you any level of internal struggle.

What if I also told you that you have the power to release *all* your emotional pain from the past and present and to stop creating it in the future? In other words, you have the power to stop self-creating negative emotions and live free from emotional pain, starting today and for the rest of your life. That is what it means to become *emotionally invincible.*

Let me share with you a story about the time I realized that we all have the choice to be completely free from negative emotions, no matter how difficult our outer circumstances may be.

When I was twenty years old, a whole lot of emotional adversity came crashing into my world. As I was driving home after giving a speech at a Cutco sales conference, my car was hit head-on by a drunk driver traveling more than 70 miles per hour and broadsided by another car traveling at roughly the same speed. It wasn't the drunk driver's car but the second car, which struck my driver's-side door, that did most of the damage. Thankfully, no one else was injured. I, unfortunately, wasn't so lucky.

The impact of the second vehicle crushed my car door into the left side of my body and instantaneously broke eleven of my bones, including my femur, eye socket, and pelvis in three places. Fifty minutes after the crash, I was finally cut out of my Ford Mustang by the fire department, using the jaws of life, and that's when I bled to death. My heart stopped beating for six minutes. Thankfully, I was revived and airlifted to the hospital, where I spent the next six days in a coma.

When I finally awoke from the coma, my doctors told me that I would likely be confined to a wheelchair for the rest of my life. (Not the best news to wake up to.) I was in disbelief. That's hard to hear for anyone at any age. But for me, at twenty years old, I just thought, *This can't be happening; I've got a lot of goals that involve walking.*

I took a deep breath, let go of that initial knee-jerk response, and thought again about what the doctors had just told me. In that moment, in my hospital bed, I remembered that I had both the responsibility *and* the opportunity to choose my response. I could choose a response that would discourage and disempower me, such as *This isn't fair. I don't deserve this. I hate that this happened to me. My life is ruined.* Or I could choose a response that would encourage and empower me, such as *I can't change this. There's no point in feeling bad about my circumstances. I have so much to be grateful for. My life is whatever I make of it.* I had the choice either to resist my reality and hold on to my negative thoughts and emotions or to accept my reality unconditionally and be free from my emotional pain. I chose the latter.

I decided to accept my new reality unconditionally: *I have been in a car accident, broken eleven bones, and suffered permanent brain damage, and the doctors believe I will never walk again.* I came to that acceptance in the span of five minutes.

*Five minutes? I don't believe it!* you might be thinking to yourself. Or maybe you're being proactive and wondering *How did he do that?* Well, for the eighteen months leading up to my accident, while working in my sales position, I had been unknowingly conditioning my brain for that moment. *Acceptance* (the opposite of resistance) had become my emotional default.

## THE FIVE-MINUTE RULE

While in my hospital bed, I immediately became present to something that Jesse Levine, my first manager at Cutco and a true Miracle Maven, had taught me in my initial training. It was called "The Five-Minute Rule," and it basically stated, "It's okay to feel bad when something doesn't go according to plan, but not for more than five minutes." Jesse taught us to set a five-minute timer on our phones anytime we experienced a failure, a disappointment, or any other unwanted result and give ourselves five minutes to feel bad about it.

We could bitch, moan, cry, complain, vent, punch a wall— whatever we felt like doing—for five minutes. Those five minutes gave us the space to feel our emotions, but the time limit prevented us from dwelling on any given adversity for an extended, unnecessary, and unhealthy period of time. It kept us from falling into that emotional black hole where most people continue reliving negative emotions that cause them to feel bad.

When the timer went off, Jesse taught us that we were to say the words "Can't change it" out loud, to acknowledge that if we can't change something, then resisting it—spending emotional energy on it and wishing it were different—is not only pointless but painful. It creates internal emotional suffering but does nothing to change the event that you perceive to be the cause of your suffering.

When I first learned the Five-Minute Rule, I remember thinking, *Uhh . . . five minutes? I'm going to need a lot longer than five minutes to be upset when something goes wrong!* Then I started applying it. One of my customers would call and cancel their order, and as soon as we hung up I would immediately hit the five-minute timer on my phone. I would pace and curse and be consumed by my negative thoughts and emotions. I would resist whatever had happened, wishing that it didn't. Then the buzzer would ding. And you know what? Just as I had expected, I was still upset! *Five minutes is not enough!* I would yell inside my head. But I kept at it, and surprisingly, within just a few short weeks, everything changed.

I would set the timer on my phone, begin pacing and cursing, and then pick up my phone to see that I still had another four minutes and seventeen seconds left to be upset. However, armed with the new awareness that it was my choice whether I continued to resist my reality or chose to fully accept what was now in the past and out of my control, I started choosing acceptance. I thought, *Why spend the next four minutes upset, when I can spend them doing something proactive that will move me forward?* I had begun building up my emotional invincibility, so to speak, and was able to choose unconditional acceptance that much faster.

The Five-Minute Rule is so effective because it makes one lesson about emotional pain crystal clear: *It's not the experience, circumstance, or event that causes our emotional pain, but rather our unwillingness to accept life as it is and move forward that's the cause.*

It's when we dig our heels in and say, "This can't be happening!" that we are flooded with painful and unproductive emotions. This is true of any time frame, whether something took place five minutes, five months, or five decades ago. For as long as you resist and wish it were different, you will continue to create and perpetuate emotional pain. The moment you accept it, you will be free.

Back in the hospital bed, I took my five minutes to be in disbelief over my new reality. Then I reminded myself that I couldn't change it, so there was no point and no value in resisting it. I made the conscious choice to accept it—fully. Yes, in five minutes. Now, if you're thinking *This is easier said than done*, it is. Everything is easier said than done when it's new to us. Remember, I had been practicing the Five-Minute Rule for a year and a half before my accident, which was why I was able to apply it so quickly. And even if it had taken me five hours or five days, the choice to accept my circumstances exactly as they were served me much better than wishing they didn't happen and letting them affect me negatively for the rest of my life.

For the next couple of days, lying in the hospital bed, I thought about my new reality. I thought about living in a wheelchair and how I would get into and out of cars. How I would do my job. How I would date. Lots of stuff. And I kept coming to the same conclusion: *I have so much to be grateful for, and my life can be whatever I choose to make of it.*

## THIS WON'T MAKE YOU HAPPY

Now, let's get one thing straight. I wasn't *happy* about the prospect of being in a wheelchair for the rest of my life; I was *at peace* with the fact that it might very well happen. There is a huge difference.

Many philosophies point to happiness as our ultimate goal. There's nothing wrong with happiness. I like being happy. However, happiness is an emotion, and emotions are fleeting. Have you ever been happy, and suddenly an unpleasant conversation changed that? You can be happy one minute and upset the next. So maybe happiness isn't the be-all, end-all that we think it is.

I've titled this section "This Won't Make You Happy" because when something undesirable occurs, accepting it doesn't mean you're going to be happy about it. Personally, I wasn't happy that I had been in a car accident and told I would never walk again. I wasn't happy later on when I was diagnosed with cancer and given an exceptionally grim prognosis. Hitting bumper-to-bumper traffic when I'm running late to a meeting doesn't make me feel happy. Thankfully, acceptance does something for us that is much more powerful than just feeling happy.

Consider that there are two general types of emotions, *positively* charged and *negatively* charged. Positively charged emotions, such as happiness, joy, excitement, gratitude, love, and the like, create a pleasant energy within us that makes us feel good. Negatively charged emotions, such as fear, anger, jealousy, regret, and resentment, create an unpleasant energy within us that makes us feel bad. In the space between positively charged emotions and negatively charged emotions is the realm of *inner peace*, and that's what we're after. Inner peace is not an emotion. It's a state of being. It's not emotionally charged, positively or negatively. It's neutral.

Inner peace is a level of consciousness or, more accurately, *con-*

*scious awareness*, and it is the space from which we can choose any emotion we want to experience at any given moment. Inner peace gives us the emotional space to create whatever we want, and is the starting place for creating miracles. It is an unwavering state of being that you can access anytime through the doorway of acceptance. It's dependent only on our willingness to make the decision to accept unconditionally all situations and circumstances in our lives that are unchangeable and out of our control. In other words, acceptance is the key that unlocks the door to emotional invincibility. Accepting everything that was out of my control (the car accident, my broken bones, brain damage, living in a hospital, the possibility that I might never walk again, not to mention the permanent scarring across my face, arm, torso, leg, and a whole lot more) gave me inner peace, free from any self-created emotional pain. Through acceptance, releasing any resistance and unnecessary pain created a space to focus all my energy on what I could control, to create the best life I could imagine, despite my new unintended and unimaginable circumstances.

Evidently, at least according to my doctors at that time, this is not the way most accident victims process news like what I had been told. Most people automatically resist their new reality and see what's lacking. They white-knuckle the visions of the life they thought they would have and believe they should have and let their negative emotions consume them. That's what is considered "normal." As we learned in chapter 3, our brains are wired to scan for danger and focus on it. We're kind of set up for this negative emotional state anytime something happens that lands outside our individual expectations. And really, if anyone were ever to be entitled to a free "I'm going to feel negative pass" about a situation, I think it's safe to say that for any of us, getting hit head-on by a drunk driver and told you're never going to walk again puts you toward the top of that list.

Though I had moved on in my new reality, my doctors were still stuck in the paradigm of how most other patients process traumatic events. As the story goes (and as it has been relayed to me since), approximately three weeks after my accident and about a week since I had woken up from my coma, my psychiatrist, Dr. Lebby, greeted my parents at the hospital and motioned for them to come into his office.

"Hello again, Mark and Julie. Thanks for coming in today. I just wanted to give you an update on how Hal's doing, both physically as well as mentally and emotionally," he said as my parents sat down across from him. He went on to explain that physically, I was doing very well. "I know it's been an unimaginable couple of weeks for Hal and for you. But I do believe he's made it through the worst, and I don't see any reason why he won't live a long, healthy life."

My mom began to cry. My dad's eyes welled up, and he wrapped his arm around my mom's shoulders and hugged her.

Dr. Lebby continued, "But we do have one concern that we'd like your help with. When assessing his mental and emotional state, we believe that Hal is in a state of denial." He went on to explain to my parents that he believed this to be true because every time that he or any of the hospital staff interacted with me, I was *always* happy and upbeat. I cracked jokes and made them laugh every chance I could. "I've been working with accident victims for many years," he continued. "And although Hal's behavior isn't really normal, it can be fairly common for someone who has been through such a traumatic experience to have trouble coping with their new reality. Most likely, Hal is suppressing painful emotions such as sadness, fear, anger, or depression." He explained that I might be doing it consciously, not wanting to experience those emotions. Or it might be completely unconscious. "Either way," he said, "those emotions will eventually make their way to the surface and he'll have to face reality at some point. We'd much rather have him do it here in the hospital, where we can monitor him and help guide him through reconciling his painful emotions, rather than let him do it on his own, down the road, when it could lead to depression or even something worse."

My parents had been under the impression that I was handling my accident with a genuinely positive attitude. Now they were finding out that my positivity might have been delusional. They both inched forward in their chairs.

"What is the 'something worse' that you're referring to?" my father asked.

"Well, it's not uncommon for accident victims to respond to their trauma by turning to various vices as a distraction or temporary relief from their emotional pain. Developing addictions to drugs or alcohol is very common, and suicide rates among accident victims are significantly higher." Dr. Lebby explained that he wasn't saying I would definitely go down that road, but he thought that the best thing for me would be to come to grips with how I was really feeling so that my doctors could guide me through the process of dealing with my emotions before I left the hospital.

"So what can we do to get Hal to open up about these emotions that you think he's suppressing?" my mom asked.

Dr. Lebby said that he would like my parents to talk to me and find out how I was *really* feeling. He wanted them to reassure me that it was normal to feel sadness, fear, anger, or even depression. He wanted to make sure I knew it was safe to express those emotions in the hospital.

Later that day, my father walked into my hospital room. I was sitting up in my hospital bed, wearing my oversized hospital gown and watching *Oprah* on the 28-inch hospital room television that was mounted on the wall. I could see a forced smile on my dad's red face and tears in his swollen eyes, and I immediately sensed that something was wrong.

"How are you doing, Hal?" he asked as he took a seat at my bedside.

"Great, Dad. Why? What's up?" I studied my father's face, trying to get a clue to what might be coming.

My father explained that he knew I was getting along okay when I had visitors around, but he wanted to know how I was *really* feeling when I was alone, thinking about the accident and what had happened to me. Was I sad? Scared? Angry? Or depressed?

I listened and nodded, though I was taken aback by his questions.

He told me about my doctor's concerns and sympathized with me by saying that he understood I would feel scared about the possibility of never walking again, depressed about my situation, or angry with the drunk driver. He said any feelings that I was experiencing were completely normal and it was okay to feel them.

I was silent for a moment as I gave serious consideration to his questions. *Am I feeling sad . . . scared . . . angry . . . or depressed? Am I in denial and covering up these painful emotions, which the doctors deem to be "normal" for someone in my situation?* Considering that I had spent the last six days, since coming out of the coma, processing my new reality, it didn't take me long to articulate the way I was really feeling.

"Dad, I honestly thought you knew me better than that."

My father raised his eyebrows but said nothing.

"You know I live by the Five-Minute Rule, right?"

My father nodded his head. "Sure, I think I've heard you talk about it before."

"Well, it's been almost two weeks; I'm way past my five minutes."

My father chuckled. I went on, "I'm way beyond feeling bad about something I can't change. Instead, I'm choosing to be grateful. After you showed me those pictures of my mangled Ford Mustang, I'm grateful to be alive! I believe everything happens for a reason, but I also believe that it's our responsibility to decide what those reasons are. So now, it's up to me to figure out what I can learn from this experience and how I can do something positive with it."

I assured my dad that I wasn't in denial. In fact, it was much more the opposite: rather than being in denial about my reality, I had fully accepted my reality—past, present, and future—so it had no control over my emotional state. If the doctors were right about my never walking again, I decided that I could either be depressed about that or be grateful for everything I still had in my life. Either way, I was going to be in a wheelchair. I told him, "I've already accepted that as a possibility and decided that if I am in a wheelchair for the rest of my life, I am going to be the happiest and most grateful person you've ever seen in a wheelchair!"

I also reasoned that although it might not be probable, it was still possible for me to walk again. Bear in mind that I was not resisting what the doctors had told me, nor was I in denial. I simply considered that walking again was a possibility that the doctors weren't counting on, because the odds were slim. I didn't know if or how it would happen, but I was committed to doing everything in my power to move my goal of walking from possible . . . to probable . . . to inevitable.

So I envisioned myself walking. I prayed about it. I thought about it. I talked about it. I maintained Unwavering Faith that it was still possible. And I went to physical therapy every single day. And when my physical therapist said we were done, I asked—sometimes insisted—that we do more. That was my Extraordinary Effort. Three weeks after my car accident, you could say that a miracle occurred. Doctors came in with X-rays of my broken leg and broken pelvis. They told me and my parents that they didn't understand how, but my body had healed in just three weeks since the crash, to the point where I could take my first step *that day*. And I did.

I believe that it was because I had chosen to fully accept what I couldn't change, my circumstances as they were, which had freed me from all emotional pain and allowed me to focus my energy on what I wanted. Unconditional acceptance had provided the emotional invincibility that helped make it possible for me to create the tangible, measurable miracle of walking again.

## RELEASING EMOTIONAL PAIN FROM YOUR PAST, PRESENT, AND EVEN FUTURE

Many people I've coached or spoken to after one of my speeches understand this concept intellectually but struggle with wrapping their head around whether or not it will work for them. Years of emotional pain have become their norm. They wonder, *How can I accept this horrible [fill in the blank] situation that I'm now dealing with?* Their shoulders are usually pushed up to their ears and their eyes are dim when they talk to me. I can tell that whatever their challenge is, they are genuinely struggling. Their pain is deep.

I explain that there is only one cause of emotional pain, which can be summed up in one word: *resistance*. Simply put, **all emotional pain that we have ever experienced, are experiencing now, or will ever experience in the future is self-created by our resistance to our reality.** Resistance typically shows up in the form of wishing and wanting something to be different that can't be. It might be wishing that something did or didn't happen in the past, resisting something that is currently happening, or worrying (another form of resistance) about something that may or may not happen in the future. And it is the degree to which we resist our reality—the degree to which we wish or want something that is out of our control to be different—that determines the degree of emotional pain we experience.

Think about it: If you're stuck in a long line at the coffee shop, and you've got somewhere else you need to be, you might have a relatively low level of resistance to the unchangeable pace of the people working behind the counter. You will experience some degree of negative emotion, which will be equal to your degree of resistance, such as annoyance, impatience, or frustration. On the other end of the spectrum, let's say you were unexpectedly fired from a job that provided financial security for you and your family and you had no backup plan. The degree of resistance you would experience regarding that reality would likely be much more intense than the resistance you have toward running late. You would likely feel anger, resentment, hopelessness, or fear of the unknown.

Regardless of the level of pain created, in both of these theoretical instances we mistakenly think that the cause of our emotional pain is the event we're experiencing. However, it's never the event that is the cause; it's our response/resistance to the event. Evidence of this is the simple fact that the same tragedy can befall two different people; and one person resists the event, deeming it the worst thing that's ever happened to him or her and claims it's going to ruin his or her life, while the other person accepts it, deciding that he or she is going to learn, grow, and become better than ever before *because* of the tragedy. Same tragedy, but two different responses that produce two very different emotional experiences.

**The only way never to experience unwanted emotional pain again is to make a conscious decision to accept everything that has ever happened or will ever happen to you.** I've even applied this to my own death, which you can do as well. Like many people, I used to be terrified of dying. But then I realized that it was pointless to fear anything that is inevitable. Birth and death are two sides of the same coin, so to speak. By accepting all of the things you can't change (death definitely fits that category), you give yourself the gift of being at peace with life as it as, rather than creating pain because you want the unchangeable aspects of life, be it your past, present, or future, to be different. Remember, you don't have to be *happy* about the things you can't change. However, you can accept them, be at peace with them, and eliminate a lifetime of unnecessary emotional suffering.

## ACCEPTANCE IN ACTION

When I began my speaking career, I spoke primarily on college campuses. Two weeks after giving a speech in Toronto, Canada, I received an email from Devon Taylor, a twenty-seven-year-old woman who had attended my presentation. Attached to the email was a photo of her wrist, displaying a tattoo she had gotten that day of just three words—the three words I had taught in my speech: CAN'T CHANGE IT. Reading her email brought me to tears and further opened my eyes to the universal power of acceptance.

She had gotten the tattoo that day because it was the tenth anniversary of her father's death. To paraphrase, she told me that she had spent the ten years since her father's death deeply depressed, in and out of therapy, and on antidepressants. She had been living under the impression that she was depressed because her father had died, and everyone in her life had reinforced that belief. Sentiments such as "You poor thing. I can't imagine how you feel" had led her to believe that she was *supposed* to feel that way, even years after her father had passed.

In her email, she went on to explain that when she heard me talk about acceptance, the Five-Minute Rule, and the "Can't change it" mantra, she started to consider that maybe the cause of her depression wasn't her father's death. Instead, maybe the reason she had been deeply depressed for ten years was that she had constantly resisted the reality of his being gone. No one had ever told her that she could consciously choose to accept that her father had died, stop resisting reality by wishing it hadn't happened, and give herself peace.

She said that the previous two weeks, after hearing my speech, had been the first time in nearly ten years that she hadn't been depressed. And that every time she had started to feel those familiar, painful emotions overtaking her, she had paused, taken a deep breath, uttered the words "Can't change it," and chosen peace instead. She had decided to get a CAN'T CHANGE IT tattoo as a permanent reminder that she would no longer allow the memory of her dad to cause her pain. Instead, she consciously chose to replace the emotional pain with a deep sense of gratitude for the time she did have with her dad.

## CONSIDER THE FOLLOWING

**You can't accurately judge an experience as "good" or "bad" in the moment.** Our resistance begins with our interpretation of an experience as "good" or "bad," and we resist experiences that we deem to be bad. However, it is often impossible to judge whether an experience is good or bad when it is happening or soon after. Often our greatest adversity becomes our greatest teacher and the cause of our most beneficial growth. Personally, I've always seen my car accident as being one of the best things that's ever happened to me because it made me stronger and was the catalyst for my life's work as an author and speaker. Literally the day I was diagnosed with cancer. I told my wife, Ursula, "This will be the new best thing that ever happened to me." It often takes the passing of time, combined with reflection and hindsight, to see the value in our challenges. For example, you could have a relationship end and be devastated, putting yourself through weeks or months or years of agony, only to find the love of your life and end up being grateful that your previous relationship ended so that a better one could take its place. It's often said that hindsight is 20/20. Sure. But why suffer now and wait until some point in the future to learn and grow from your adversities in the present? Unconditional acceptance gives you the space and freedom to be at peace with your challenges almost immediately (or at least, in five minutes).

**There are no problems.** There is no such thing as a problem. The word *problem* is a label for a situation. There are merely situations, which become problems only if we choose to view them that way. We can choose to label any given situation as a problem or an opportunity or "to be determined" or any other label we choose. The label we assign to each of our situations creates our perception and experience of it. Want to cause yourself stress and make life more difficult than it needs to be? Label all your undesirable situations as problems and just keep piling them on top of your existing problems. That will keep you too busy to create a Level 10 life.

**You can't accurately judge emotions as "good" or "bad."** Emotions are inevitable. We are humans, and humans are emotional creatures. If someone wrongs you, you're probably going to initially feel anger, sadness, disappointment, or frustration toward that person. If you were to lose a loved one, you would naturally feel sadness, despair, or a general sense of loss. All of these emotions are natural. Our objective is not to eliminate negative emotions but to change your relationship with them.

Our initial emotions aren't the problem; it's what we do with them beyond the initial feeling that can make or break us. If you experience something that causes you to feel any sort of negative emotions, but then quickly accept it, are at peace with it, and move on with your day, then you're good. The problem is our judgment and ongoing resistance of the emotions. Though our initial resistance to our reality is what triggers emotional pain, it is our judgment of the emotion as "wrong" and subsequent resistance that keep us stuck in that negative emotion and perpetuate our pain. We keep flipping back and forth between judging and resisting. And that hurts emotionally.

When we judge our emotions as "bad" or "wrong," we amplify the effect that the emotion has on us. Have you ever woken up feeling sad for no apparent reason and then heard your inner voice chime in with *Why do I feel this way? Something must be wrong.* Before you know it, your moment of sadness has turned into a near meltdown. *Maybe I'm depressed!!!* The more we focus on a feeling and then judge ourselves for it, the worse we feel.

Negatively charged emotions shouldn't be viewed as the enemy. In fact, there is value in all emotions. If you lose something or someone important to you, feeling sad and grieving are not only natural, they can be healthy. And sometimes we need to feel the pain that resulted from a choice we made so that we won't make that choice again. The distinction here is for you to be in control of your emotional state, rather than allowing circumstances and events that are out of your control to dictate your emotions.

**Don't wish for a perfect life tomorrow. See the perfection of your life today.** Another thing that we do is to strive for perfection (guilty) and then measure our reality against our vision of what we think our reality should be. This, too, is simply another form of resistance. You are focusing on the lack, resisting your actual reality against your perceived perfect reality, and thereby creating emotional pain. You can just as easily choose to view your life through the lens of *My life is perfect just as it is, right now.* When I had cancer and was enduring the most difficult year of my life, one of my favorite mantras became *My life is always perfect. I am always exactly where I need to be to learn the lessons that will enable me to create everything I want for my life.* I couldn't change my diagnosis, so I chose to accept it, be at peace with it, and make a conscious decision that I would be the happiest and most grateful I had ever been while I was enduring the most difficult time in my life. I chose to view my diagnosis, and the lessons that inevitably came, as part of the perfection of life. You can do the same in the midst of your challenging circumstances.

When people hear me tell the story of my car accident and how I fully accepted my circumstances from my hospital bed, they are usually skeptical or surprised that I'm not at least angry with the drunk driver. "How could you not hate him for what he did to you?" some people ask. Sometimes they're even angry for me. But I don't hate him. In fact, I have absolutely no negative feelings toward him. If I've felt any emotion toward him, since the accident and to this day, it's *empathy.*

You see, I never lived his life. Perhaps, in his shoes, I would have made the same choice to drink and drive that night. It's easy for us to judge others, based on our life experience and who we are. However, think about someone you've judged or been upset with, either currently or in the past. Consider this: *If you had lived his or her life, been born with his or her brain, been raised by his or her parents and influenced by his or her friends, there is a very high probability that you might think and act exactly as he or she does.* From that perspective, we can choose to replace our judgment with empathy and to love all people unconditionally. We can accept them as they are, while simultaneously holding space for them to become the best version of themselves.

Another common question I get is *How do you know what you can and can't change?* The simple answer is *You can't change anything that's ever happened.* You can only make changes to your actions now, which will lead to different circumstances in the future. Your past and current circumstances are fixed. In this moment, only your future is malleable.

You can't unflood your basement filled with water. You can't undent your bumper after your fender bender. You can't actually take back something you or someone else said. Once it's occurred, it's occurred, and you can't go back in time and change it. I mean, unless you're Marty McFly with a time-traveling DeLorean.

When you accept the past unconditionally, you let go of resentment, regret, anger, guilt, and any other negative emotions that your resistance has created. When you accept every unknown event that will one day happen to you (aka *accept life before it happens*), you release all of your fear, anxiety, worry, and other forms of emotional pain that are completely unnecessary.

To give yourself the gift of inner peace and become emotionally invincible, you must release all resistance to whatever has already happened or will ever happen, no matter how painful it was at the time or how frightening the possibility of something happening in the future may be. You do this by accepting your reality unconditionally, as it is. Here are the three techniques that you can use to accept all things that are out of your control and give yourself the gift of emotional invincibility.

1.  **The Five-Minute Rule:** Applying this was my first step in this process. Set your timer and give yourself five minutes to feel your emotions, fully. Kick, scream, cry, complain— whatever you have to do to exercise those emotions. As soon as the timer goes off, accept the situation by speaking three very powerful words . . .

2.  **The "Can't change it" mantra:** Remind yourself that you can't change what's already occurred—whether it happened five minutes, five months, or five decades ago— and thus there's no value in wishing you could. You can't undo the past, nor can you alter the unchangeable aspects of your present or future. Understand that if you can't change a situation, continuing to resist it will only generate more unnecessary emotional pain. You have the power to stop that pain or never to experience it in the first place.

Know that you may have to repeat these two steps a few times when you first begin in order to break your emotional patterns.

3.  **Accept life before it happens:** This is the evolution of acceptance and will be much easier for you once you've practiced the Five-Minute Rule and the "Can't change it" mantra for a period of time. Now that you're aware of the fact that all emotional pain is self-created and completely

optional, you can prevent emotional pain in the future by consciously deciding now that you will never again resist anything that you can't change. You don't need to endure emotional pain for any period of time, only to look back and realize it was unnecessary. Don't wait for hindsight to find your peace. Accept life before it happens to be at peace always and in all ways.

In the next chapter, we are going to explore a whole new paradigm for setting goals and how you can use it to eliminate your fear of failure forever. But before we move on, I would love for you to sit with this notion of emotional invincibility for a few minutes. What causes you emotional pain? How would accepting everything that's ever happened or will ever happen to you change your life? How much more energy do you think you would have in the absence of stress, anger, sadness, and any other prolonged negatively charged emotions?

Let's put the rubber to the road and test this idea out in your life. Consider this question: What's *your* wheelchair? What is the circumstance in your life or your past that's unchangeable, yet you resist it and thereby create unnecessary emotional pain?

Now take a deep breath and make the conscious choice to accept it unconditionally, be at peace with it, and give yourself the gift of becoming emotionally invincible.

5

# A NEW PARADIGM
# OF POSSIBILITY

Your Goal Is Not the Goal

The major reason for setting a goal is for what it makes you do to accomplish it. This will always be a far greater value than what you get.

—JIM ROHN

We all have dreams, grand visions of what our life could be like. These visions make us feel good when we think about them. We imagine what's possible. At times we even venture into a bit of goal setting or action planning that can move us in the direction of achieving those visions. Yet few people actually set meaningful goals for themselves, and even fewer actually achieve their goals. Just consider those New Year's resolutions that peter out before January even ends.

The sad truth is that most people's real life never matches that grand vision. That million dollars never materializes. The person of our dreams never walks through our door. Our dream job never falls into our lap. And so we're left to perpetually wish for things we believe are out of reach. And the more time passes and the older we get, the worse that feels.

There's gotta be a better way.

What if you were to operate from a paradigm in which you could not fail? What if you knew that every goal you attempted would come to fruition?

Would this paradigm change the way you approach your goals? Would you shoot higher? Take more risks? Feel more motivated?

From my vantage point, our current relationship with goals seems a little off. The way we approach our goals leads us to one of two possibilities: either we reach our intended result and succeed, which usually makes us feel good; or we don't reach our intended result and fail, which usually makes us feel bad. After all of the goal setting and figuring out the baby steps we need to (hopefully) achieve our intended result and then following those steps until the end, we still have only about a fifty-fifty chance of succeeding (or failing) when all is said and done. That doesn't sound very motivating to me.

That actually sounds kind of demotivating. It sounds like a paradigm that nudges you in the direction of either keeping your goals small, so that you're sure to reach them, or not even trying, so that dreaded failure isn't possible. Putting in all that time and effort without any kind of guarantee feels as though it might be a waste of your time, right? When our goals start to feel improbable or start to look like too much work or as though they will take too long, it's easier to simply go back to our comfy couch and dig around for the remote control—again.

I see how this paradigm limits so many people. Before I understood the fail-or-succeed paradigm, I, too, was guilty of buying into this limiting way of looking at goals. I didn't realize it then, but I was keeping my goals small to avoid failure—until I realized that I was just as worthy, deserving, and capable of achieving anything I wanted as any other person on the planet. And so are you. But we must think about goals in a different way if we are ever going to make our mark on the world. Thanks to one of my mentors, I did actually find what I was looking for: a whole new way to approach goals, one that removes the possibility of failure.

The remainder of this chapter will ease you into your new relationship with goals, one in which your success will be inevitable. We will first redefine the real purpose of a goal, which will open you to thinking about what's possible for you in a much bigger way while simultaneously removing the debilitating fear of failure that we all have to overcome.

## THE REAL PURPOSE OF A GOAL

Everyone wants to achieve his or her goals and dreams. That's probably why you are reading this book. We also know that it's in our nature to look for the easiest path to achievement. The low-hanging fruit isn't necessarily the most exciting, but it is what most of us shoot for. Before we put much effort into a goal, we want some sort of guarantee of success. If you're an optimist, you likely abide by the optimist club's credo that "anything is possible." However, we rarely pursue that which is possible and instead focus our energy on achieving what we believe is *probable*.

Think about it: When was the last time you pursued a goal that you didn't really believe you were likely to achieve? You probably thought it would be a waste of time, not worth spending your energy on it or setting yourself up for failure and possibly embarrassment. I mean, who goes after goals that they don't believe are achievable? That seems kind of pointless, right? Well, if you are under the impression that the highest value of setting a goal is to reach the goal, then, yes, by all means shoot for the low-hanging fruit. But reaching a goal, as in the tangible result, is not the ultimate purpose, nor is it the most significant benefit, of setting a goal. It's not the highest value. In fact, in this new paradigm, whether or not you reach a goal is inconsequential to the true purpose of your goal's endgame.

Stay with me here.

The real purpose of every goal you set is to become the type of person who can consistently set and achieve significant goals. In other words, the purpose of a goal is to develop the qualities and characteristics of a goal achiever. It is *who you become* through the process that will serve you for the rest of your life and trumps any short-lived achievement. Ultimately, you want to use each of your goals to develop the mindset and behaviors of a Miracle Maven. You get there by applying the Miracle Equation to each goal, over and over again, thereby making your long-term success inevitable. Each goal is simply an opportunity to develop yourself and to test what is actually possible. And the more we do this, the better we become at it.

I'm going to repeat something that we touched on in chapter 2, and that is what my mentor Dan Casetta taught me about goals. Again, this is a lesson handed down to Dan from one of his mentors,

Jim Rohn. To paraphrase: *The purpose of setting a goal is not to hit the goal. The real purpose of setting a goal is to develop yourself into the type of person who can achieve your goals, regardless of whether you hit any particular one or not. Some goals you'll reach, and some you won't. It is who you become by giving it everything you have until the last moment—regardless of your results—that enables you to develop the mindset and behaviors that will help you achieve bigger and bigger goals for the rest of your life.*

## YOUR GOAL IS NOT THE GOAL IN ACTION

You may be familiar with Lewis Howes. I interviewed him years ago on my *Achieve Your Goals* podcast, and he was featured in *The Miracle Morning* documentary. He has a fascinating story. He is one of the best examples of someone who has exemplified the real purpose of a goal.

Lewis's primary goal in life when he was younger was to become a professional athlete. He did actually achieve this goal. He played one season of Arena League football before he got hurt. Not only did his career come to a grinding halt, but so did his life.

Lewis had no backup plan. He was broke and floundering. He had no idea what he wanted to do in life. He had never considered any other goals. He knew he had to figure something out, though, so he began by reaching out to a bunch of influencers, interviewing and learning from them. One mentor told him to check out LinkedIn, which was relatively new at the time. He spent hours every day studying the site until he had built up his own profile enough that others began asking him to help with theirs. He simply followed his passion and curiosity until the world realized that he was contributing something special. That passion and curiosity eventually led him to podcasting.

Fast-forward several years, and Lewis is now one of the best-known podcasters in the world. He hosts a top 100 podcast, *The School of Greatness*, which boasts more than 40 million downloads. He authored a *New York Times* bestselling book and was recognized as one of the top one hundred entrepreneurs in the country under thirty by the White House and President Barack Obama. His media appearances are likewise impressive; he has been on *The Ellen DeGeneres Show* and the *Today* show. He has also been featured in *Forbes, Inc.*, and the *New York Times*, to name just a few.

Now Lewis's mission is to share "greatness" around the globe and empower people to change their lives; to help others uncover their gifts and offer their own unique contribution to the world. The mindset and work ethic he developed on his way to his goal of becoming a professional athlete was his key to achieving much bigger goals, far outside the realm of what he had ever imagined for himself. Lewis isn't living out the life he intended. His goal when he was younger really wasn't his goal. Still, the lessons he learned put him into a position to be a Miracle Maven. His miracle now is helping others create their own miracles.

## YOU CAN NOW RELEASE YOUR FEAR OF FAILURE

Once you understand and embrace the real purpose of a goal, you realize that failure is nothing to be feared, because you cannot fail. Who you're becoming is always more important than what you're doing, yet the irony is that it's what you're doing that is always determining who you're becoming. As long as you maintain Unwavering Faith and put forth Extraordinary Effort with each and every goal you set, regardless of your results, you will always learn, grow, and become more capable than you were before. And your future goals, including those you have yet to even imagine, will reap the rewards.

I would also like to point out that this does not let you off the hook when you encounter an obstacle on the way to your goal. I'm not saying that it's okay to give up if you see that the probability of reaching your goal is unlikely. Remember how my push-period story in chapter 2 ended? It literally took until the last possible moment for me to hit my sales goal. And it played out similarly for most of my colleagues who applied the Miracle Equation. Their miracle came to fruition in the last week . . . on the last day . . . even in the final hour. I'm not sure exactly why that is, but it does seem to be consistent. Time and time again, I've seen or experienced that the universe seems to test us continuously to see how committed we are to achieving our goals. While most people give up along the way, only those who are committed to maintaining Unwavering Faith and putting forth Extraordinary Effort until the last possible moment get to see their miracles come to fruition. Those final moments are critical and were what brought me to another level of what I could create in my life. Not reaching your goal when you have given it everything you could until the last possible moment is very different from giving up when things don't look as though they are going to work out the way you planned—because in reality, no one reaches all of the goals he or she pursues. Not even Miracle Mavens.

I have a poster hanging in my son's bedroom that displays a famous quote from Michael Jordan: "I've missed more than 9,000 shots in my career. I've lost almost 300 games. 26 times I've been trusted to take the game-winning shot and missed. I've failed over and over and over again in my life. And that is why I succeed."

Failure is a foundational part of the learning process. It's how we grow. When you approach goals this way, even if you fail to reach your intended target, you will never fail to achieve your highest purpose.

If you've maintained Unwavering Faith and put forth Extraordinary Effort but fall short of your target, you've still developed the qualities and characteristics of a Miracle Maven, which will enable you to consistently achieve your goals moving forward—characteristics such as faith, self-discipline, work ethic, resiliency, and more.

## ONLY THE GROWTH LASTS FOREVER

Normally I like to use real-life examples and stories to illustrate lessons, but in this case, I think the following hypothetical scenario will best illustrate how this new paradigm plays out. Let's begin with two colleagues, John and Mary. They were both in their early forties and earned middle-class incomes working for medium-sized companies. Both dreamt of becoming millionaires.

One sunny afternoon, John stopped into the local convenience store and bought a lotto ticket while paying for some snacks. Luck was on John's side that afternoon, because he hit all five numbers and instantly went from an angsty office worker to a millionaire man of leisure. The next morning, he quit his job, went looking for a much larger house, and purchased a six-month luxury vacation across Europe. Life was looking good for John.

Fed up with her career, which hadn't advanced in years (and with no winning lotto ticket), Mary decided to leverage her experience and started her own consulting business. She put her heart and soul into it, not to mention a large chunk of her 401(k). But, like most businesses, it failed within a year. Mary took a step back and wondered if she should try again or go back to an office job that she hated but that would, at least, offer a steady paycheck.

Within that same year, John returned from his extended vacation and moved into his mansion—alone. He purchased several new cars and filled his time watching television during the day and going out to restaurants and bars most nights. He felt bored most of the time but kept hoping that another purchase or fun night out would make him feel better.

After careful reflection, Mary decided not to go back to another job that she hated. She tapped into her Unwavering Faith and started over with a new business. Using the lessons she had learned from her first failed attempt, she gained some traction in the marketplace and started making money. It took nearly ten years, but she did, finally, reach a million dollars in her bank account. And that money only continued to grow as she scaled her business over time. She never gave up, regardless of the results she saw along the way. Mary became a Miracle Maven.

Unfortunately, those ten years were not as good for John. John's spendy ways led him to bankruptcy court. Sure, John had acquired a million dollars a lot faster and easier than Mary did. But he had no idea how to hold on to the money. He didn't respect his winnings, nor did he develop the qualities and characteristics that would enable him to grow his fortune or at least hold on to it.

Though these are imaginary people, these circumstances (usually in smaller proportions) happen all the time. Most of us are impatient. We want results immediately. But *immediately* is not a great time frame for the self-development necessary to attain and maintain worthwhile results. It's simply not enough time to develop the qualities you need to achieve, let alone sustain, success. That's why we see so many people to whom success comes quickly, from lottery winners to overnight celebrities, lose their fortunes as fast as they acquired them.

## HOW OUR PARADIGM EXPANDS

Both as a species and individually, human beings' ability to continuously expand what's possible is quite remarkable. Many times over, what once seemed like a fantasy has become our reality, which led to expanding our identities and creating greater possibilities for our future.

Consider that when you were an infant, walking was not possible. Then eventually, you took your first step, and suddenly walking became your norm. Then you started to run and skip and eventually mastered jumping. The milestones seemed to unfold naturally for most of us and got closer together as we aged. This is a lot like how our identities expand and take shape.

We went through a similar process as we moved through school. In elementary school, the thought of being a middle schooler was a dream. Then, as we entered middle school, the possibility of one day becoming a high schooler seemed almost too good to be true. Those kids were so cool and grown-up!

When your first day of high school finally arrived and you stepped onto campus as an incoming freshman, you became one of those cool high schoolers. However, as a freshman you weren't nearly as cool as the seniors. They were older, most of them drove cars, and some of them were already taking college classes.

Think back to when you were a freshman and how much older and more mature you perceived the seniors at your high school to be. I can still remember how I viewed the seniors who attended Yosemite High School with me. Not only were they supremely cool and seemed to be significantly more mature than I was, but they also seemed to have it all figured out.

Now when I remind myself that those supremely cool, seemingly more mature seniors who "had it all figured out" were still teenagers and were actually just as supremely immature, insecure, and confused as I was during my senior year of high school, I'm reminded that we all have the potential to attain the level of those we admire. Whatever future may seem like a fantasy to you now is simply a future reality that you have yet to create.

One of the most telling examples of how we're able to continuously expand our paradigm of possibility is when it comes to how much money we're capable of earning. As kids who were excited just to collect loose change that we could stockpile in our piggy banks, the idea of earning $10 was outside the realm of possibility for most of us. Once we began receiving payment for chores or were hired by a neighbor to mow the lawn, we upgraded from stockpiling change to accumulating dollar bills. Suddenly, $10 entered our realm of possibility and we set our sights on our next target: earning $100. Eventually the possibility of earning $100 increased to $1,000, which eventually grew to $10,000, and so on.

I vividly remember being nineteen years old and giving up my dream job as a radio disc jockey, who earned a meager $10 an hour to play music and give away concert tickets, to try my hand at a "commission only" job, selling Cutco cutlery. My first week, I earned more than $3,000 in commissions, which would have taken me more than three hundred hours to earn working at the radio station. As you might imagine, to earn in one week what would previously have taken me nearly four months created a new paradigm of possibility for my financial future.

I had the unique opportunity to interview dozens of self-made millionaires when I was writing one of my most recent books, *Miracle Morning Millionaires: What the Wealthy Do Before 8AM That Will Make You Rich*. A common theme was how their financial possibilities gradually and continuously expanded over time and continue to do so.

For most millionaires, earning $100,000 in a single year was once a fantasy for their younger self. When they finally achieved that previously elusive six-figure income, it became their norm, and they set their sights even higher. For most, what followed was a gradual climb—both internally in terms of beliefs and externally in terms of income—from $100,000 to $200,000 to $300,000, and so on. Each new level of income provided a new paradigm of possibility as the next level came into view. It's also interesting to note that their work level didn't necessarily increase with their income. Often it even decreased. As they became more knowledgeable, more experienced, more efficient, and more effective, they also earned more money. Their wealth was a result of who they had become.

## UPGRADING YOUR PARADIGM

There is some debate over how many thoughts we think each day. I've seen several numbers tossed around the internet, with the most common in the 50,000 to 60,000 range. Regardless of the number's accuracy, I think we can all agree that we do, in fact, think *a lot* of thoughts each day.

The exact number of thoughts is inconsequential. What's more important is for you and me to acknowledge that the majority of our thoughts from day to day are the same. This becomes critical when you consider that our thoughts create our identity. In other words, whatever you consistently think about yourself becomes your reality. You are as capable or as incapable as you think you are. The possibilities for your life are as limited or as limitless as you think they can be. It's all in your perception. We wake up, and our minds are flooded with habitual thought patterns, often guided by the chronology of our day. We think about what we have to do to get out the door in the morning. All day long we think about what's on our schedule. Then we think about what needs to be done when we get home and before we go to bed. We give ourselves little to no time to consider a bigger future and clarify who we need to be to create it, and so our life stays the same, because we stay the same.

When we keep thinking the same thoughts, we are confined to the same possibilities or lack of them. The reality we are living now has and is being created by the thoughts that we've allowed to consume our minds up to this point. To improve your life, you must first improve what you habitually think about. The most effective way to do that is to craft *written* statements (so that you're not relying solely on your memory) that are strategically designed to guide and focus your thinking on what matters most to you, what's possible for you, who you need to become, and what you need to do in order to make what's possible *inevitable*. We will be spending a substantial amount of time on how to do this in chapter 9.

All Miracle Mavens begin by being willing to see themselves as better than they have ever been before. When you do this, you realize that what you have or haven't done in the past no longer matters. Your thoughts matter, and when you take control of your thoughts and you own that responsibility, you understand that your ability to create meaningful results and improvements in your life is always present. Coupled with a consistent process, your chances of achieving greater success move into reach.

## THE YEAR THAT CHANGED EVERYTHING

Before I left Cutco, I set one more goal for myself—a quantum leap—to *double* my previous best year in sales. Increasing your sales by 25 percent or 50 percent is intimidating, but trying to increase my annual sales by 100 percent was downright terrifying. I had spent the previous seven years, during my late teens and early twenties, working toward a milestone of selling $100,000 of product in a single year. And I did hit that goal twice, which got me into the company's top ten (number five and six) each year and earned me company trips to Cancún, Mexico, and Banff, Canada.

In 2004, at age twenty-five, I was ready to move on to pursue my dream of becoming an author and a keynote speaker. But as I was about to move on, I had a painful realization: I had never fulfilled my potential as a sales representative with Cutco. Selling $100,000 was a part-time effort, and I had never given it everything I had, at least not for an entire year. I wanted to double my best year ever and shoot for $200,000 in a single year—a milestone that had only been achieved by a handful of sales reps—with my primary purpose being to develop the qualities and characteristics that would enable me to achieve everything else I wanted for my life. That goal became my *mission*.

It's not that I didn't have any other goals that year. In fact, I committed to more significant goals (in terms of quality and quantity) than I ever had before. In addition to doubling my best year ever in sales, I also set out to write and publish my first book, give twelve speeches in high schools and colleges, work out five days a week, rock climb three days a week, meet the woman I would eventually marry, and donate $10,000 to charity. And though these were my main goals, that isn't even the whole list. I had goals for every area of my life.

Clarifying which single goal was most important and making

it my mission for the year made a tremendous impact on the way I went about achieving both it and all of my other goals (we're going to work on determining your first mission in the next chapter). Becoming clear on which of my goals was my top priority—selling $200,000—automatically prioritized how I spent my time. Simply put, I didn't allow myself to spend any time on my other goals until I had followed through with the predetermined process that would make achieving my mission virtually inevitable.

In order to double my annual sales, I doubled the number of calls I made each day (my "process"), and I completely removed my emotional attachment to the results of those calls and the sales presentations that followed. I simply followed through with my process, which would inevitably get me to my desired result. I also formed and led a team of my colleagues each of whom shared the same goal of hitting $200,000 in sales that year. Every week, we all jumped on a call together and shared our wins, our setbacks, and our most valuable lessons. Although that was on my longer list of goals, forming the team actually supported my main mission. As I ventured into new territory, this team gave me support, new ideas, and a lot more energy whenever I started to slump and doubt myself.

Less than twelve months after I set my goal, I received my commission statement in the mail and saw that I had generated just over $205,000 in sales for the year. I stared at the number almost in disbelief. I remember standing at the foot of my bed and then just falling backward, as if in slow motion. It felt as if I were falling onto a cloud (insert inspirational music). My pulse quickened as my brain tried to process that I had achieved what I had considered to be highly improbable. It actually took a few minutes for my new reality to supersede my old. From that vantage point, I realized we all have the ability to overcome our fears and achieve anything that we're willing to commit to.

And I wasn't the only one. Five others on my team also hit the $200,000 goal, which was the most in company history. But that's not the end of the story. The interesting thing that happens when you become hyperfocused on a singular goal and you approach that goal with Unwavering Faith and Extraordinary Effort is that you'll also achieve other goals that you thought you'd left behind simply because they align with your new identity.

In the span of that one year, I also wrote and published my first book, *Taking Life Head On: How to Love the Life You Have While You Create the Life of Your Dreams*; launched my paid speaking career; got down to 5.7 percent body fat (I don't even know if that's healthy); met the woman of my dreams (with whom I now have two kids); worked out five days a week; rock climbed three times a week; started practicing yoga; and donated more money to charity than I ever had before. It was truly the year that my entire life changed, because I changed my paradigm, both of what I was capable of and what I was committed to. In short, after years of accepting less than my best, I had finally expanded my own potential and become a better version of myself. That year was one of the best of my life because I stepped up and became the person I always knew that I was capable of becoming. And that's the experience I'm excited for you to have, as well.

As we move into the next chapter, I invite you to consider this new goal paradigm in the context of your own life. Can you think of any times when you gave up early or never even got started, because you believed that success was improbable? How about a time when you pushed through that doubt (or logic) and ended up surprising yourself? We all have these stories. There have been plenty of times in my own life when I worked really hard and hit the goal. There have been times when I didn't work that hard and still hit the goal. There have been times when I worked really hard and didn't hit the goal. And there have been times when I didn't work very hard and didn't hit the goal. The point is that your effort doesn't always translate into success in terms of tangible results. But it will *always* translate into your developing yourself into the person you want to be.

Now that we have tackled what the real purpose of a goal is and expanded your paradigm of possibility, the next chapter is going to dive even deeper and lay out how to determine what matters most to you. You'll figure out which of your goals will become your mission— your single most important goal that will have the greatest impact on your fostering the qualities and abilities of a Miracle Maven.

# 6

# YOUR MISSION

It's Time to Get Clear About
Your Top Priority

Your work life is divided into two distinct areas—what matters most and everything else. You will have to take what matters to the extremes and be okay with what happens to the rest. Professional success requires it.

—GARY KELLER

S o how does it feel to consider this new paradigm of possibility? Now that you understand the real purpose of a goal in a whole new way, you can begin setting goals as big as you want, goals that really matter to you, and there's no longer anything to fear, because you *cannot* fail. You can only learn, grow, and become better than you've ever been before. The farther outside of your comfort zone you go, the more you'll learn, the faster you'll grow, and the sooner you'll embody the qualities of a Miracle Maven. A world of limitless inevitabilities is now open to you.

Maybe you have even allowed yourself to daydream a little about what your life would look like (and feel like) as you start living this way—if you increased your income and established an unshakable level of financial security, upped your exercise and got into the best physical shape of your life, and *finally* started checking off the items on that seemingly forgotten list that houses your biggest goals and dreams. Wouldn't life be great? Especially if your biggest goals and dreams came to fruition all at once.

Hold up a minute, there. All at once? Were you thinking that you would tackle *all* of your biggest goals at the same time? Let's talk about this for a minute.

## THE POWER OF SINGULARITY

Over the last twenty years, as I have worked with people from all walks of life, a common obstacle I have seen is that most of us are trying to work on too many goals at once, with no clarity as to which of our goals deserves top priority. We have health goals, family goals, financial goals, work goals, relationship goals—the list goes on and on. You know what happens when we fail to prioritize our goals? We stay busy, perhaps make some inconsequential progress, but almost always end up with missed targets and/or feeling overwhelmed.

We can compare this kind of goal setting to multitasking. It's so easy to get caught up in taking on too many things at once. We're culturally conditioned to go through our days like this, splitting our brain up to perform different tasks, seemingly at the same time. We quickly check a notification from Facebook while we are working. We talk on our cell phone while we drive. We read through text messages while we play with our kids. We seem to have conquered multitasking. But are we really more efficient?

The simple answer is no. A 2009 Stanford study found that people who often multitask using several different forms of media are actually less effective. They have more trouble screening out nonessential information and switching between two different tasks. Their memory is also not as sharp as that of those who do not shift their attention while working.* Multitasking slows down your progress. And pursuing several goals, with equal importance assigned to each, does the same thing.

Let's say you divide your focus among five separate goals simultaneously. In a few months' time, maybe you will make 5 to 7 percent progress on a couple of the goals, while others trail behind at only 2 to 3 percent and some you haven't touched at all. Over a few more months, you might make another 5 to 7 percent progress on some, 2 to 3 percent on others, and completely avoid at least one or two. After six months, you've barely scratched the surface of each goal. By then you've likely lost the initial drive and motivation that you began with when you set each goal, and you'll be tempted to move on to five new goals that are fresh, stimulating, and exciting. If you take the same approach, you'll make another 5 to 7 percent progress (or less)

---

\* Eyal Ophir, Clifford Nass, and Anthony D. Wagner, "Cognitive Control in Media Multitaskers," *Proceedings of the National Academy of Sciences of the United States of America* 106, no. 37 (2009): 15583–87, https://doi .org/10.1073/pnas.0903620106.

on your new five goals. This approach of dividing your focus among too many goals becomes a never-ending perpetual cycle of failed goals and unrealized potential. It also prevents you from developing the ability to prioritize, focus, and remain focused over an extended period of time, which are crucial to achieving significant goals and creating tangible, measurable miracles.

The more goals we set and give equal priority to, the less likely we are to achieve what matters most to us. If we're not crystal clear on our highest priority (singular), human nature leads us to stay busy by pursuing the path of least resistance and engaging in the activities with the least significant consequences. We send an email when we could be more effective making a phone call. We watch Netflix when we could be reading a personal development book. We allow our busyness to usurp our limitlessness.

We need to stop doing this. It's time to learn how to focus on what matters most to you so you can start experiencing more of what really matters. So in this chapter and the remainder of this book, you are going to focus on one goal—your most important one, the one that will make the most significant impact on the quality of your life. I realize that might feel unsettling. "But Hal," you say, "lots of things are important to me. I have many goals that I'd like to achieve. How do you expect me to choose just one?" I hear you. And I understand how counter this feels to our whole multitasking culture. But I really want you to succeed in becoming a Miracle Maven, and you'll find that establishing and maintaining a singular focus is the most effective way to do that.

Priceline.com founder and billionaire Jeff Hoffman recently spoke at one of the Quantum Leap Mastermind retreats that my business partner, Jon Berghoff, and I cohost, and of the many takeaways that I wrote down, the following stood out most: "You can't win a gold medal at more than one [sport]." Let that sink in for a minute.

Most Olympic athletes spend their entire lives focused on developing themselves to be best in the world at one thing. And remember what we learned in the last chapter, that when you choose and commit to one mission, achieving your other goals will become more probable, because you will be living in alignment with your highest priority.

In this chapter, you're going to come clean on whether or not you are living in alignment with your top priority. (Chances are you're not. Don't worry, you're far from alone in that.) Then you are going to take the plunge and commit to one singular mission (and I would urge you to do that while reading this chapter, when all the material is fresh in your mind) before I offer up some safety nets to ensure that achieving your mission is something you can count on. This will all be in preparation for your first Miracle Equation 30-Day Challenge in chapter 10.

Okay, take a deep breath. We're diving in.

## START WITH WHAT MATTERS MOST

Some would say that the fastest way to identify your top priority is to come face-to-face with your own mortality or the mortality of someone close to you. When I was diagnosed with cancer at age thirty-seven, I thought my priorities (yes, I had multiple priorities at that time) were, number one, family; number two, health; number three, friends; number four, financial security; number five, productivity/achievement; and number six, fun—in that order. However, being told I had a 70 to 80 percent chance of dying in the coming months revealed what you may soon realize is true for you, as well: I was delusional.

If you had asked me what was most important in my world, I would have told you, without hesitation, "My family." And I meant it.

There was nothing and no one I loved more than my wife and our two children. They were my world. And I truly believed that all my other priorities lined up behind them, that everything I did was for them.

So what was the problem? Where was the disconnect? Well, it wasn't hard to spot the disconnect with a quick scan through my schedule. The way I chose to spend my time told a very different story: I went on frequent business trips, I worked sixty-plus hours a week, I gave up family time on the weekends because I had yet *another* big project due. If my family were really my number one priority, they sure got pushed aside—and often for my supposedly less important priorities. My actions were simply not lining up with what I was saying (or even believing) was most important to me.

Upon deep introspection and reflection, it turned out that I valued productivity and my achievements above everything else. Almost all of my time and energy went into finishing one project and securing the next. Instead of focusing on my children's bedtime story, I was preoccupied with my business metrics. Instead of listening to how my wife's day had been, I'd give her the obligatory head nod while I scanned my emails and responded to those I deemed urgent. I wasn't really focused on any single thing—especially not on my family. But I had good reasons. At least I thought I did. I valued financial security for me and my family. I wanted those people, who meant more than anything else to me, to be well fed, well clothed, and comfortable. When I sat back and examined that line of thinking, though, I saw that my focus on financial security didn't stem from my love for my family; it stemmed from fear. The subtle shift in my priorities had nothing to do with them at all.

In the years following the economic crash of 2008, I went from what I thought was having complete control over my finances to losing more than half of my clients, who were suffering the effects of the crash themselves and could no longer afford to work with me. I couldn't pay my mortgage with the big dent in my income, and I ended up losing my home in foreclosure and ruining my credit. That was my rock bottom, and it was terrifying. Nothing I did to try to drum up business worked, and I just kept spiraling farther and farther into debt. I was really at a loss for how I was going to dig myself out of the financial hole I was in. Even though I did ultimately turn my situation around and start moving forward, I realized years later that I was still driven by a deeply ingrained fear that I could lose it all again.

And so every email from a client became paramount. Every keynote speech I gave was like a lifeline. Yes, I did want to provide for my family. More than that, though, I was afraid of going through a financial crisis again; the depression; the place of feeling as though I had zero control over my life.

To combat that fear, productivity had become my top priority, whether I was aware of it or not. And talking to countless people after my speeches this year, I see that this is the case for most of us. Whether you call it productivity or success or accomplishment or work, they all fall into the same bucket and many of us are literally addicted to it. Not only do we focus on tasks that keep us busy and aren't highly consequential, but we focus on them to the detriment of what matters most to us.

When we work nonstop in this way, it is damaging to both our bodies and our brains. So right there, we are undermining our own health. Looking even further, we also undermine our family, our fun, our spirituality, and even our work (all at the same time) because we will ultimately burn ourselves out. If you really can have only one top priority, everything else is automatically bumped down the list.

But we don't do this only with productivity-related tasks, we do it with lots of activities that just aren't that important. Consider how much time you spend bingeing on Netflix or watching the news, surfing the internet, checking Facebook, or even playing games on your phone. Yes, all of these count against the time you spend on your highest priority. If you have ever thought, *I don't have enough time to get to my top priority every day*, it's not necessarily that you don't have enough time but more that you are spending your time on lower-priority activities that you are thinking of as high priority simply because you spend so much time doing them. Remember, your schedule never lies.

It wasn't until my cancer diagnosis that I realized not only that I was living out of alignment with my top priority but also that I was living every day driven by fear. Sure, I had good reason to live that way based on what I had been through. But I don't think any of us want to live our lives driven by fear; I know I didn't. So I decided to make some radical changes so that my top priority, which was my family, actually came first. It all started when I came home from my first five-day chemo session, I sat in front of my then four-year-old son and said to him, "Buddy, we can do anything you want today! We can go to the lake. We can race go-karts. We can go bowling. We can do *anything* you want!"

His response: "Really? Hmm . . . Let's play with my toys in my bedroom!"

I thought he must have misunderstood me. "No, buddy, I said we can do *anything* you want! If you could do anything, what would you want to do?"

His response: "I just want to play with you in my bedroom."

That was really eye opening for me. I realized that my son's top priority was simply to play with me. If family was really the most important thing in the world to me, then what was most important to my son had to be most important to me.

In a flash, I had a simple but profound realization: My kids aren't going to remember how many mortgage payments I made. They aren't going to care how many books I sold. And at the end of my life (which I hope won't be for a long time), neither will I. I also realized that by waiting until after work to spend subpar "quality" time with my kids, I was giving the most important people in my life "leftover Dad." They weren't getting the best version of me. They were getting me when I was tired, worn out, and mentally drained. And so were they. I had to flip that around so that my family actually came first in my schedule, both literally and figuratively.

So before my son and I went and played in his bedroom that morning, I scheduled a thirty-minute recurring timer to play with my son first thing in the morning, before he left for school. It cost me nothing but a bit of time, and it meant everything to him. And we've been able to deepen our connection every day, as a result.

## ALIGN YOUR SCHEDULE WITH YOUR TOP PRIORITY

Since that day with my son, and after recovering from cancer, I've been hyperfocused on my family and extremely intentional about being the best father and husband that I can possibly be. That focus has led me to make radical changes to my schedule so that it is aligned with my highest priority and what truly matters most to me. Here's what a typical day/week now looks like in our home:

I still wake up every day at 4:30 a.m. to do my Miracle Morning and the S.A.V.E.R.S. For my "R" (Reading) time, I now have a rule that I'm not allowed to read a business book until I've read at least ten pages out of a parenting or marriage book. This commitment alone reminds me every day that my family is my number one priority.

At 6:00 a.m. I head into my son's and daughter's bedrooms to wake each of them up (something that my wife used to *always* do while I continued my isolated morning routine). I try to wake my kids up in a way that starts their day with a positive mindset and positive emotions. First, I usually crawl into their beds and cuddle or tickle them. Then I speak words of affirmation as they're waking up, such as, "Good morning to my favorite son/daughter. . . . You are kind, loving, and intelligent. . . . You are being filled with positive energy right now as you wake up. . . . It's time to get out of bed and make today your best day ever." I just say whatever comes to mind. Often I will sing their affirmations, sometimes in a funny voice, just to mix things up and make waking up enjoyable for them.

Once my kiddos are dressed and teeth brushed, we do a "kid-friendly" version of the Miracle Morning. Then I still play with my son (his favorite thing to do), which has evolved from playing with action figures to playing board games. After our kid-friendly Miracle Morning and a little playtime, I basically act as my wife's personal assistant, helping her pack lunches and get the kids ready for school (something that, again, I *never* used to do, because I was hidden away in my office working). Helping my wife and kids get ready in the morning is now a meaningful family experience. It's not an obligation, but an opportunity to deepen our connection and for me to positively influence my children.

Next, I take my son and my daughter to school (something I also used to mindlessly delegate to my wife). That quality time together every morning with my kids—setting their intentions for the day, having meaningful conversations, listening to upbeat music and dancing (yes, we have dance parties in the car)—has been priceless! I also started getting off work at 2 p.m. instead of 5 p.m., three days a week, so that I can pick our kids up from school. It was difficult to carve those three hours out of my workday at first, but I am so glad that I did.

Around 5:00 p.m., we have dinner together as a family, at which time we each take turns playing the Gratitude Alphabet game, saying what we're grateful for, starting with something that starts with the letter A. I'm also part of the kids' bedtime routine. I read them a bedtime story or tell them a story from my childhood (which, by the way, is a great way to let your kids get to know you *and* teach them valuable lessons that you've learned throughout your life). This also ensures that I am bookending my day with my top priority—spending time with my kids first thing in the morning and last thing before they fall asleep.

On Saturdays, I take the kids for a Daddy-Kiddo Fun Day, which gives us another opportunity to spend quality time together doing something that brings them joy *and* gives my wife a day to herself. And every week, my wife and I are religious about keeping our "date night." We get a babysitter and head out to get some quality time together.

All of these changes didn't happen overnight, but gradually. And they definitely weren't easy to make. I still have a deeply engrained fear that the economy could crash again and I could face another personal financial crisis, which only reinforces my addiction to work/productivity. The good news is I've found that the longer you stay committed to living in alignment with your top priority (as it is with any change), the easier and more natural it feels. The other day, someone invited me to an event that could be significant for my business, and without hesitation, I said, "No, thanks, I'm with my kids that day."

I'm also far from perfect, as some days I still have to bow out and tag my wife in. But the biggest breakthrough with regards to my relationship with my top priority—my family—is that I am no longer willing to spend "enough" time with them to check off an imaginary box for the day. Instead, while they're young and still want to spend time with me (which more experienced parents have warned me will end sooner than I'd like it to), I am committed to spending as much time with them as humanly possible. My number one priority in my life is to connect with and positively influence my children, and the only way to do that to the fullest is to spend quality time with them. The more I'm with them, the more we deepen our connection and the more I can positively influence their development. So I'm running toward that time every chance I get.

I wish I were alone in my years of not living in alignment with what truly matters to me, but after sharing my new (postcancer) keynote message "What Matters Most" with thousands of people, I know that I was part of the majority. If you fall into this category, the most important thing for you to do is to acknowledge it and commit to making changes. Be honest with yourself. If you want work to be your priority, then commit to it and don't feel guilty about it. Before I had a family, I was great with work being my top priority. Some days work is still my top priority, but that is now the exception to the rule. If you know your health needs to be your primary focus, make sure that your actions and your schedule support that choice.

Know this: your top priority can and will change. I'm sure you don't have the same priority now as you did when you were fifteen years old. And it will change again, maybe several times, over the rest of your life, so don't put too much pressure on yourself when it comes to figuring out what your top priority is right now. And don't be afraid that all your other goals will suffer because of this choice. What you'll find is that once you get clear about what your top priority is and what matters most to you, your productivity will actually increase.

## WHAT MATTERS MOST TO YOU?

Can you say with certainty that you are clear about what is most important to your life? Is it family? Friends? Your health? Your purpose? If you're not sure, I invite you to endeavor to find out, as the most successful, most fulfilled people on Earth are those who have clearly identified what matters most to them (aka their highest values and top priority) and they live every day in alignment with what truly matters.

I do realize that not everyone has a life-altering event crash into their world that sets them up to see more clearly what's most important to them and how they want to live in alignment with that value. So if you're still trying to figure that out, let's try a different approach.

Let's travel to the future for a moment and imagine that you have been living as a Miracle Maven. You now wake up and approach every day with Unwavering Faith and Extraordinary Effort. You are consistently creating results that leave you feeling accomplished and fulfilled. People now look at *you* and think, *Geez, everything just flows for them. They're so lucky!* You're the happiest you've ever been and at peace, because you are living in alignment with your highest values and your greatest abilities. And your schedule proves that. Although you see opportunities everywhere, you're able to say no to most of them, because you only capitalize on those that are in alignment with what you've decided is most important to you.

When you see this Miracle Maven version of yourself, what do you value most in life? Is it family, health, work, finances, spirituality, fun, contribution, or personal development? How do you know this? Which activities in your schedule support your highest values and your top priority?

I realize that I'm belaboring this point, but identifying what you value most is going to be essential to clarifying your mission. Miracles—especially the tangible, measurable kind—are much easier to attain when you are living in alignment with those values and top priority. Otherwise, you'll feel as though you're constantly being overwhelmed by the delusion of multiple priorities and torn about where to focus your energy at any given time.

Now, if you're clear on your top priority, pull out your list of goals that you have written down. If you don't have any goals already written down for your year, life, and so on, please put this book down now and take a few minutes to jot down some goals that you would like to move toward in the coming months. Don't worry about making them perfect; just get started with the first thing that comes to mind (that you'd like to improve) in each of the following areas:

- Health and fitness
- Family
- Friends
- Work
- Money

- Fun
- Personal development
- Spirituality
- Contribution/charity

As you review your goals to determine which is important enough to be your top priority, answer this question: **Which *one* of these goals will enable me to develop the qualities and characteristics that I need to achieve everything else I want for my life?**

This goal should propel you toward the Miracle Maven vision you had of yourself, based on the qualities and characteristics that it would instill in you; qualities like discipline, resilience, consistency, and most important, Unwavering Faith and Extraordinary Effort. Does this goal align with the top value that you aspire to live by? If not, consider if either the goal or the value should change. Remember, you want all of your focus and energy flowing toward your new identity, so your top goal and your top value should be in sync. Also, don't back away from goals that seem intimidating or too difficult to achieve. It's normal for a top goal to intimidate or even scare you. It should be out of your comfort zone. It's going to force you into a new way of being, so make sure it's significant.

Would the goal of losing a substantial amount of weight require you to develop the qualities and the identity of a Miracle Maven? How about starting a business? Changing careers? Writing a book? Running a marathon? Or doubling your income? Those last two are the ones that did it for me.

Once you are clear about which goal will most effectively carry you toward this new identity, it becomes your *mission*. I use the word *mission* intentionally (in my own life as well) because it evokes a more serious tone and suggests a higher purpose. By Merriam-Webster's definition, a goal is "an end toward which effort is directed." Setting goals is fun. You get to imagine all these great things happening. And if they don't, you just choose some new goals and have fun imagining them coming true. They end up being more like fantasies.

A mission, on the other hand, implies a different level of commitment. One hundred goals will never carry the weight of a singular mission. The military carries out missions. Humanitarian organizations carry out missions. The weight here is much different from that of a goal, and the objective is usually attached to a larger vision. Different language here will create a different experience for you.

**Goals:** Many things we *want* to accomplish.

**Mission:** *One* thing we are *committed* to accomplishing, no matter what.

Remember, to decide on your mission (if you haven't already), look at all of your goals and answer this question: **Which *one* of these goals will enable me to become the person that I need to be to achieve everything else I want for my life?**

My mission is: _____

_____

_____

_____

_____

Now that we've built up a bit of momentum by clarifying your mission, don't panic on me. *But how am I supposed to accomplish this huge goal?* you may be wondering. We aren't going to lay that out quite yet, but I promise we will walk through how to develop your process in chapter 8. I'm going to tell you right now, it will be much easier than you might think. So let's keep things moving.

## CREATE YOUR MISSION SAFETY NETS

If you are an aspiring tightrope walker (I'm not either), before you ever step onto the wire, the first thing you make sure you have in place is a safety net. The same is true when you're attempting anything that is new, scary, and outside your comfort zone.

Your first hurdle when it comes to creating a miracle is establishing Unwavering Faith (which we'll cover in depth in the next chapter). The more we can inch your mission toward probable, the more likely you are to get engaged and stay engaged with it. Before you plunge into your mission, here are a few strategies you can start working on to increase your chances of accomplishing it.

## Establish Monthly Missions (Accomplish More Every Thirty Days Than Most People Do in Twelve Months)

Every New Year is an exciting time for goal achievers. It provides us with an opportunity to reflect on our progress in the previous year and set new goals for the coming twelve months. However, every year, millions of goal achievers set annual goals, and every year, most fall short in one way or another. Why is that?

I once read an excellent book, *The 12-Week Year*, which opened my eyes to the perspective that a year is a long time—maybe too much time? Not on track for your goals by the end of January? Not a big deal; you still have eleven months to get back on track. How about when you're still not on track in April? No worries, you've still got May, June, July, August, September, October, November, and December to make up the slack. Plenty of time, right?

The challenge of long-term goals is that, by giving ourselves so much time, we miss out on an invaluable sense of urgency. When procrastination is combined with an unrealistic and perpetual sense of optimism—when you are always thinking *I've got plenty of time*—delaying becomes a luxury that we mistakenly think we can afford. This cycle leads to missed opportunities, unreached goals, and unfulfilled potential.

What if, instead of giving yourself twelve months to achieve your goals, you gave yourself one? What if *every single month* your New Year began? What if every month were an opportunity to reflect on your progress, to set new goals, and give yourself a fresh start?

Establishing a monthly mission—a single goal each month that supports your larger mission—will provide you with a laser focus on your highest priority each and every month. It will also provide you with a healthy, consistent sense of urgency and keep you on track for your ultimate mission: developing the mindset and behaviors of a Miracle Maven.

## Engineer Your Environment

Without realizing it, we are often the ones placing goal-deterring obstacles in front of ourselves. We say that we want to lose twenty pounds, yet we stock our pantry with cookies and soda. We intend to meditate or exercise in the morning, yet we check our phone and get sucked into emails, social media, and our never-ending to-do list. We claim to have big goals and dreams, but the time to work on them seems to be missing from our schedule.

Evaluate your environment, and take a look through your schedule to make sure that there is nothing that will interfere with your number one priority. Ideally, "Mission Time" should be a recurring appointment in your schedule, as early in the day as possible to ensure that you tackle your most critical tasks first, because the longer you wait, the more likely you are to put them off until the next day (raise your hand if you've ever done that). It's also easiest to get through your most important tasks when you have the most energy and your head is clear. If instead of the morning, you want to hit the gym on your way home from work, keep your gym bag in your car. You can even change into your gym clothes before you leave your office. Make it easy to fulfill your goal.

If you want to secure more clients for your business, make sure that you have a set time and a quiet place in which to make phone calls and set up meetings. If your goal is to master a foreign language, make sure that you surround yourself with books, radio stations, and even people who speak that language. We've already discussed how to make emotional space within ourselves so that there is room for miracles. You need to engineer your physical space as well.

Also, consider the people with whom you surround yourself. If you are surrounded by people who make a lot of excuses and never seem to get anywhere in life, you aren't going to gain much motivation from them. Look for people who are already doing what you would like to be doing or at least who are living in alignment with their top priority and achieving success, whatever that may be.

Now that my schedule is aligned with my "family" mission, it's essentially on autopilot. This has allowed me to refocus on my mission of remaining cancer free so that I can live a long, healthy life with my family, and I've arranged my environment to fully support that mission. Every morning, I spend ten minutes reciting cancer-free affirmations, followed by ten minutes of cancer-free meditation, followed by reading ten pages of a cancer-related book that teaches me how to remain in remission. I drink homemade organic lemon water every morning and have delicious, organic, plant-based foods delivered to me every week from Veggie Vibes (www.veggievibes.com). I invested in an ozone sauna machine, which I use three times a week, take around thirty supplements every day that have proved to help people with my kind of cancer, and do weekly coffee enemas. (I can assure you, effort doesn't get much more extraordinary than sticking a tube up your butt.) I've intentionally set up my whole environment to support my current mission in life. Like my "family" mission, my "cancer-free" mission is also now on autopilot, so I can redirect my focus to another mission. As you align your schedule and engineer your environment to support each mission, eventually you too will reach an autopilot phase and be able to redirect your focus to your next mission. And as you develop the qualities and characteristics of a Miracle Maven, you tend to reach autopilot faster and more easily each time.

## Establish a Resource for Accountability

I know how easy it is to get stressed and give up when you are trying to do something you've never done before. Reaching out and surrounding yourself with like-minded individuals is a worthwhile pursuit. Here's why: assembling and leading a team provides you with accountability, encouragement, and perspective, all of which can be invaluable in helping you achieve your mission.

First, you hold one another accountable for doing what you say you're going to do. One of the most powerful and underutilized resources available is *integrity,* which I define as *doing what you say you're going to do, when you say you're going to do it, without exceptions or excuses.* When you commit to living with impeccable integrity, you gain the power to speak your life into existence, because if you say you're going to do something and you keep your word, it's as good as done (also known as *inevitable*).

In reality, maintaining integrity all the time is easier said than done, especially since one of our default modes of action is searching for excuses. In fact, although we usually do it unconsciously, we tend to value our excuses above our integrity. How can you assess whether or not you tend to look for excuses? Consider what happens when you aren't on track to meet a deadline that you've committed to. Where do your focus and creativity go? Instead of putting forth Extraordinary Effort to meet the deadline no matter what, your default (which you might not even realize) might be to think up excuses that you hope will get you off the hook from your commitment, so that you can delay the effort, or eliminate it entirely. What began during childhood as "my dog ate my homework" becomes nothing more than a slightly more sophisticated attempt to dodge responsibility. Don't feel bad if you realize that you do this. Most people do. And that's why it's so important to surround yourself with people who are equally committed to fulfilling their potential and achieving significant goals: they create a safety net of sorts. They can hold you accountable for doing what you said you would do or call you out when you are resting on an excuse.

They also serve as support and encouragement. Let's face it, there is no straight path to any goal. There will be ups and downs, good days and bad days. And when you have enough bad days and feel like giving up, having a built-in support network will be vital to your success. It's like having a whole group of personal coaches dedicated to you. But this doesn't work only one way. Providing support for others also brings out the best in you. Holding others accountable tends to help you be more accountable.

Your team of Miracle Mavens (or whatever you want to call them) can also offer up different approaches and strategies when you get stuck, and vice versa, that can accelerate your gaining the clarity that will move you from being stuck to getting unstuck. Simply not being alone also takes a lot of the fear out of a huge goal. And being surrounded by a group of like-minded people, each with his or her own playbook of what has and hasn't worked, is invaluable.

If you don't know a group of like-minded people who are also working toward significant goals, or if you don't like working in a group, the next alternative would be to find an individual accountability partner. He or she can perform the same functions as the group, as long as you have a recurring time to talk and the other person is rigid enough to hold you accountable to your process. Two of my Miracle Morning coauthors, Cameron Herold (*The Miracle Morn-*

*ing for Entrepreneurs: Elevate Yourself to Elevate Your Business*) and Joe Polish (*The Miracle Morning for Addiction Recovery: Letting Go of Who You've Been for Who You Can Become*) are each other's accountability partners. They check in daily with each other and facilitate their shared accountability using a goal-tracking app called CommitTo3, which calls on them to clarify their top three objectives each day and make sure that they follow through. The point is, just make sure you have someone else to support you and to ensure that you uphold your impeccable integrity. I would strongly suggest that this person *not* be your spouse, a family member, or a loved one because they are likely to let you off the hook more easily than someone not as close to you. Put some time into your schedule now to start recruiting, as this single factor can make or break your success.

### Be On the Lookout for Your Miracle Mentor(s) (You Never Know Where You'll Find Him or Her)

It's beneficial to have at least one mentor, because we're all limited to only one perspective, our own. Your mentor might be someone on your team of Miracle Mavens or even the person you've chosen as your accountability partner. While a mentor can hold you accountable, more often he or she gives you a glimpse into a wider pool of possibilities. Mentors offer advice and provide guidance. In some cases, your mentor will be able to give you advice based on his or her own experience attempting (and maybe even achieving) the very goal you are working toward. Other times, your mentor may just be someone who knows you well enough to see a path that you had never considered or felt confident in pursuing.

Jon Berghoff, whom I mentioned earlier in the book, falls into the second category of mentors. He has positively influenced me over the past twenty years and has arguably made the most profound impact on my life. When we met, though, he was the last person I imagined would ever become my mentor.

First of all, he was younger than I. Second, we began as bitter archrivals at Cutco. He was hired a year and a half after I was and quickly began breaking nearly every sales record I had set with the company. I still remember our first awkward meeting at a sales conference, just minutes after he had taken down my precious push-period sales record. Over the next year, we started getting to know each other, and we eventually became great friends. Turned out that he was one of the most brilliant people I had ever met, which is partly why he was able to outsell every sales rep in the history of our company (including those with decades of experience) despite being younger and less experienced than all of us.

In 2001, while still selling Cutco, I was recruited by another company to sell its product part-time. I thought it would be a good way to diversify my income and I called Jon to see if he wanted to join me at the other company as well. His response, although unexpected, completely changed the trajectory of my life.

"Hal, what are you doing?" His voice was serious. "Listen, man. You died, and you were told that you would never walk again, but you did. I know you don't think it's a big deal because it's just what you did and it's what came naturally to you, but it's not normal." He told me that I should share my story and teach people how I had responded to my adversity and how I had overcome it, so that they could do the same. "If I were you, I would be investing every spare minute I had into writing a book about your story, not selling another company's product." I thought about what he said to me and realized that he was right. That conversation became the catalyst for my life's work as an author and keynote speaker.

When I met Jon, the last thing I thought was that he would one day be a mentor to me. That's why I always tell people to keep their ears open for good advice; it might come from an unlikely place, and that's okay. The more we seek to learn from different types of people and welcome their feedback, the more chances we have of finding new mentors and gaining new perspectives that will bring us closer to our Level 10 life.

## Make Your Mission Public

To seal in your unwavering commitment to your mission and to help you hold yourself accountable to it, make it public. Tell those closest to you what you are striving for and why you are fully committed to it, no matter what . . . there is no other option. I know there is a school of thought that tells you not to share your goal, that you should show people instead of tell them, but sharing your goal with others can make all the difference. When you don't, it's much easier to let yourself off the hook. We do it all the time.

I've seen the impact that making goals public has, because I have experimented with it several times. You know that I formed a team of other sales reps who were also striving for the $200,000 mark when I set out for that goal, which made my mission public to my colleagues and provided each of us with support and accountability. I made an even bigger public commitment when I decided to run an ultramarathon (that's fifty-two consecutive miles) for charity. Now let's get some context around this commitment: To all of the runners out there, I salute you. But I am *not* one of you. Although I'm not particularly proud of it, I do belong to the "I hate running" club. I always have.

However, in mid-2008, I committed to a mission of running an ultramarathon *because* I hate running. Sounds totally backward, I know. During one of my Miracle Mornings, I had the thought *I won-der who I'd have to become to run fifty-two miles in one day. I don't know that guy. I've never met him. I wonder what he's like.* I imagined that he was a hell of a lot more disciplined and capable than I was. Shoot, he could probably accomplish pretty much anything he put his mind to, and I really wanted to become that person.

So I did two things to leverage the support and accountability of others. First, I went onto Facebook and committed publicly to running an ultramarathon to raise money for my favorite charity, the Front Row Foundation. Making the commitment public set me up with the leverage I needed to follow through. I figured that even during those times when I felt like giving up (which we all experience on our journey to creating miracles), that I wouldn't want to be the flake who committed to raising money for charity and then changed his mind. I then went online and ordered a book, *The Non-Runner's Marathon Trainer.*

Luckily, I had three friends who were willing to do the ultra-marathon with me: James Hill, Alisha Anderer, and Favian Valencia. We dubbed ourselves "ultrafriends." In the end we all completed the marathon, and though I can't speak for my ultrafriends, *I still hate running.* But you know what I did in the process? I not only *met* that guy who could run an ultramarathon; I *became* him. And my life has been the better for it ever since. When you make a public commitment to people whom you respect, and whose respect you value, giving up is not an option.

## WHEN YOUR MISSION LEADS TO MULTIPLE GOALS IN ACTION

My friend and another former Cutco colleague John Israel (I know, if it weren't for Cutco, I wouldn't have any friends) is another great example of how following one mission led to accomplishing multiple significant goals. John, otherwise known as "Mr. Thank You," is on a mission to elevate the level of gratitude on the planet by 1 percent, one thank-you card at a time. The first year he committed to this mission, he set out to handwrite five thank-you notes a day, every single day. And they had to be to different people; he could send a maximum of three notes to any single person in a year. Interesting mission, right?

The way he approached the rest of his life goals was also interesting. All of his other goals were fed through the filter of his mission: *gratitude*. That was how he accomplished so much that year. He had a baby, moved across the country, and grew a community of like-minded "Miracle Maven" dads. Through that filter, his relationships and community expanded quickly and he ended up having his best year ever at Cutco, bringing in an impressive $445,000 in sales while achieving his mission of handwriting and sending out 1,825 thank-you cards. By giving more gratitude to the world, he ended up with a lot to be grateful for. All of his goals lined up behind his mission, which supported him in accomplishing nearly everything else that he set out to do that year.

## DON'T FORGET ABOUT YOUR OTHER GOALS

I know that we've discussed identifying and deciding on one singular goal as your highest priority, your mission. But that doesn't mean that the rest of your life needs to be left behind. It just means that your mission needs to come first. Once that's done, you can tackle whatever you want.

If you remember, the year that I doubled my best year in sales was also one of my best years in terms of reaching nearly all of my other goals. Setting a singular mission forces you to prioritize your time and focus on one goal at a time in order of what matters most, which is much more efficient and effective than waking up and working on whatever feels easiest. It can actually be much easier to achieve multiple goals when you are focused primarily on one.

Now that we've covered the real purpose of a goal and how to choose your mission, the next two chapters will dive deeper into the two decisions you must make to become a Miracle Maven and move your biggest goals from possible . . . to probable . . . to inevitable. If committing to a goal so big that it scares you still seems unthinkable, you may want to read the following pages twice.

# 7

# YOUR FIRST DECISION: UNWAVERING FAITH

You Have to Believe, Until . . .

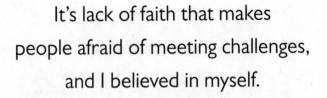

It's lack of faith that makes
people afraid of meeting challenges,
and I believed in myself.

—MUHAMMAD ALI

D id you know that

Twenty-seven publishers passed on Dr. Seuss's first book. He then went on to publish more than sixty successful titles, selling more than 600 million books globally.

Babe Ruth had 1,330 strikeouts *and* held the home run record. He is considered one of the greatest baseball players of all time.

Vincent van Gogh sold only one painting, to a friend, but kept on painting. By the time he died, he had created more than eight hundred works, which now command millions of dollars apiece.

The multitalented writer, actor, producer, and director Tyler Perry lost all of his money (and he didn't start with much) when his first play tanked. Not to be deterred, he forged on and continued to retool and stage the play while sometimes living out of his car. It took six years, but finally—*finally*—the play hit and his career continued on a meteoric rise. His net worth has since climbed into the hundreds of millions of dollars.

Walt Disney was fired from a newspaper because he "had no good ideas" before he went on to create one of the most creative companies that ever existed.

Elvis Presley was told after an audition at the Grand Ole Opry that he should go back to his job as a truck driver. He ignored that advice and went on to become a music icon.

Michael Jordan was cut from his high school basketball team before joining the Chicago Bulls and becoming a basketball icon.

Some of these stories I had heard before. A few I didn't know about until I began doing the research for this book. But I found all of them so interesting. Dr. Seuss kept writing. Babe Ruth kept swinging. Van Gogh kept painting. Tyler Perry kept restaging. Walt Disney kept imagining. Elvis Presley kept singing. Michael Jordan kept shooting baskets. But why? Why did they keep going? For many of them, success came many years after their initial attempt. Some even fell into financial ruin along the way. Each of them had to, at some point, face the same self-doubt we all face. Why—and perhaps a better question is how—did they persist when they kept meeting failure time and again?

The only answer I have been able to come up with, that is true for all of them, is that they have maintained Unwavering Faith.

As you know, the Miracle Equation encompasses two decisions that must be established and maintained over an extended period of time: Unwavering Faith and Extraordinary Effort. These two decisions, if you choose to move forward with them, radically increase your probability of achieving success. They don't guarantee your success, nor do they conjure up any magical energy that attracts your desired result to you. It's really much more concrete than that.

As each of the Miracle Mavens above illustrates, it is by establishing and maintaining faith that you can achieve something that propels you into action. And the more action you take, the more chances you have to reach success—and the more capable and effective you become along the way. As you move in the direction of any outcome that you've committed to, what's *possible* for you starts to become *probable* and over time will eventually tip into *inevitable*. That is where you'll meet your life of miracles.

What I get from these stories, and what I hope you do as well, is that success almost never falls into your lap and there are no short-cuts. The only way to keep going is to keep the faith. None of these folks (and so many more) would ever have made it to the summit of their career had they let setbacks cloud their vision and cause their faith to waver. It was their faith that fueled their ongoing effort long before they met with success. It was their decision to maintain faith that was clear, bold, and unwavering. In this chapter, we'll discuss how you can develop and cultivate Unwavering Faith as well as see it in action.

## THE LEAP INTO UNWAVERING FAITH

Faith is a bit elusive. It's hard to come by because, by definition, it requires no proof. And so it feels intangible, maybe not so trustworthy. When most people talk about faith, it's often in the context of something bad that's happened. "Just have faith that this horrible thing happened for a reason," we are told. Or "Have faith that things will turn around." I guess this kind of faith can make you feel better for a moment. Sometimes.

I'm not talking about this kind of faith. I'm referring to faith in the context of what's possible for you—your ability to overcome any adversity you face and produce tangible, measurable miracles. Which, at first blush, still feels intangible—and not so trustworthy. Because having faith requires taking a leap away from our typical skeptical nature. And really, Unwavering Faith, which is 50 percent of the Miracle Equation, is not natural. Unwavering Faith isn't something a person is born with. It's not inherent. And it's not a feeling. On the contrary, it must be consciously established in a moment of decision and then actively cultivated and maintained over time. Every tangible, measurable miracle begins with an individual's belief that manifesting that miracle is a real possibility. That faith is then maintained as Extraordinary Effort is put forth until the miracle becomes a reality, however long that takes. One of the benefits of making the decision to maintain Unwavering Faith is that it enables you to override all of your negative self-talk and gain access to a mindset that most people never experience.

Understand that Unwavering Faith is the first decision that all Miracle Mavens make and continue to make throughout their lifetime. By making that decision consciously and repeatedly, it becomes the fundamental mindset through which they view all challenges and opportunities. When people describe the mindset of any top performer, Unwavering Faith is sometimes referred to by other terms, such as extraordinary self-belief, supreme confidence, or bulletproof conviction. Regardless of what you call it, you'll likely never meet a Miracle Maven who doesn't embody this mindset.

## THE YEAR I ALMOST DIED—AGAIN

I'm not sure why my life has been tested more than once, or at all. However, I have learned that we always have the power to choose our mindset—to be genuinely happy, grateful, and optimistic, even when the world around us is falling apart. By making that choice, we're able to maintain our sanity so that we can put the world, our world, back together again.

The most recent time I used the Miracle Equation was undoubtedly the most difficult and the most rewarding. It literally saved my life. One otherwise normal evening in October 2016, I awoke in the middle of the night, gasping for air. Struggling to breathe, I wheezed loudly, which woke my wife, Ursula.

"Are you okay? What's wrong?" she asked.

"I don't know." I wheezed again. "I'm having trouble breathing." She immediately propped me up on a few pillows, which provided enough relief that I could attempt to fall back asleep. We agreed that I would drive over to the walk-in urgent care clinic first thing in the morning, and I eventually dozed off sitting upright. The following day, I walked into our local urgent care clinic hoping that the doctor there could figure out what was wrong. I was diagnosed with pneumonia and given a pack of azithromycin (antibiotics) that the doctor said he hoped would help. It didn't.

Over the course of the following weeks, things got much worse, to the point where I was checking myself into the hospital ER every other day to drain my left lung because it kept collapsing. And it was extremely painful each time. The process consisted of sticking a large needle through the back of my rib cage to drain the excess fluid. And it was a lot of fluid. During that period, I had a combined eleven liters (twenty-two pounds) drained from my lung. Yet nothing provided me with any sustained relief. Every time the fluid was drained, it replenished. Every night I struggled to sleep because I was struggling to breathe. The hospital passed me from one specialist to another in an attempt to determine what was causing my lung to keep collapsing, but no one had any answers. That is, until I saw Dr. Berkeley.

Dr. Berkeley ordered a variety of tests and scans for me, all of which I endured. The next day, his nurse practitioner called me, and with a sense of urgency in her voice, told me that Dr. Berkeley wanted to see me as soon as possible to go over my results. Finally, it was looking like I might get some answers. So I jumped into my car and drove back to Dr. Berkeley's office. As I sat in his office, waiting for him to enter, I felt relieved that I was about to discover what was wrong with me and why I hadn't been able to breathe normally for almost two weeks. Dr. Berkeley entered, sat down across from me, and began to go over my tests. The culmination of the results came in the form of his preliminary diagnosis: "Hal, this looks like it could be some kind of cancer."

*Cancer? No. That can't be right*, I thought. Not for me.

Years earlier, I had watched the documentary *Healing Cancer from*

*Inside Out.* I had followed that by reading books on health, such as *The China Study* and *Eating Well for Optimum Health: The Essential Guide to Food, Diet, and Nutrition.* As a result, for the six years preceding my cancer diagnosis, I had been living what I believed to be an "anticancer" lifestyle. At thirty-seven years young, I had been eating a primarily organic plant-based diet with small portions of grass-fed, hormone-free, high-quality meats, for more than a decade. I exercised regularly. I meditated daily. I was genuinely happy and actively maintained minimal stress. I didn't drink much alcohol, beyond an occasional beer. Ursula and I had even gone as far as removing all of the toxic chemicals from our home. Only uber-natural, chemical-free shampoos, toothpastes, deodorants, and cleaners filled our shelves. You could say that we were modern-day hippies.

So I got a second opinion from another nearby hospital, followed by a third at the MD Anderson Cancer Center in Houston, Texas. It was there that doctors quickly discovered that not only had my left lung collapsed but both my kidneys and heart were also on the verge of failing. Although I was there to determine whether or not I had cancer, I quickly found myself on a stretcher as nurses rushed me into the ER with orders to drain another sac of fluid, only this time it was surrounding my heart. The fluid was an eighth of an inch thick, and the ER doctor informed me that if the fluid expanded by just another eighth of an inch, my heart would stop beating, I would go into cardiac arrest and they would have to perform open-heart surgery.

I was in disbelief. I was terrified. And things just kept getting worse.

The doctor explained that to drain the fluid, the surgeon would have to insert a large needle into my chest, puncture the sac of fluid sitting just one-eighth of an inch from my heart, and do everything in his power to keep the needle from stabbing me in the heart. I was to be fully awake for the procedure, and before they started, I was required to sign a waiver stating that if they did accidentally stab my heart and cause me to go into cardiac arrest, I couldn't sue the hospital. I kissed Ursula, who was now sobbing, and hugged my father before two men in olive green medical scrubs wheeled me into the operating room, which had glass windows so that my family could watch the procedure.

Fifteen minutes later, it was done. No stabbing of my heart. No open-heart surgery. Yet the ordeal that would occupy the next year of my life was just beginning. We still had to figure out what was causing my organs to fail. I couldn't understand it. How could I have gone from being the picture of health to being on the verge of death in a matter of days?

The specialists at MD Anderson soon diagnosed me with an exceptionally rare, extremely aggressive form of cancer, known as acute lymphoblastic leukemia, or ALL. ALL is so rare that the previous two hospitals I had gone to didn't have the equipment to confirm my diagnosis. ALL is so aggressive that most people who die from it do so as a result of being misdiagnosed, as I was at the urgent care clinic. ALL acts so quickly that by the time most victims find out they have it, it's too late to save them. Even when it is properly diagnosed, the odds are still very grim. The prognosis for adults with ALL is a 20 to 30 percent survival rate. For any glass-is-half-empty folks out there, you might say that's a 70 to 80 percent "you're going to die" rate. One of my worst nightmares was now my reality—leaving my wife without a husband and my kids without a father. Things didn't look good.

Further testing at MD Anderson showed that my cancer contained a rare cellular mutation known as NUP1. The mutation, in combination with ALL, is so rare that there are no published survival rates. Thus, a 20 to 30 percent chance of surviving was my best hope, but one leukemia doctor told me my chances could be as low as

10 percent. When I ran a Google search for "acute lymphoblastic leukemia with a NUP1 mutation," the first mention of it didn't show up until page four of my search. There was not a single doctor or medical practitioner on the planet that I'm aware of who had had any success curing my cancer.

I adore my wife. My two young children own my heart. I had a global Miracle Morning Community to lead. I had more to lose than ever before. Cancer was by far the most terrifying and potentially devastating adversary I had ever faced. With no clear path to healing, what was I supposed to do?

The first conscious choice I made was to harness emotional invincibility by fully accepting that I had cancer. No resistance. No wishing that I didn't have cancer, because that would be delusional, pointless, and only perpetuate more emotional pain. Instead of resisting my reality and wishing it were different, I consciously chose unconditional acceptance, which enabled me to both be at peace with my diagnosis and created space for me to focus all of my thoughts and energy on the outcome I wanted, rather than the outcome that I was afraid of. Cancer was my new wheelchair, so to speak. Just as I had after my car accident, I decided that I'd be the happiest and most grateful person I could possibly be while I battled cancer and faced my unknown future.

## REPLACING FEAR WITH FAITH

As I thought about the diagnosis I had been given, it was clear that I couldn't spend my time focused on the statistical probability that I was going to die. I knew that would only trigger my stress response, which is not helpful when you are trying to heal. I decided that fear was not going to consume my cancer journey. I wasn't happy that I had cancer, but I wasn't going to let my fear aid in killing me. I would have to do something to increase my odds of living, to move those odds from possible to probable and, most important, inevitable.

I immediately recalled the Miracle Equation. It was the one thing that I knew from countless experiences could defy the odds and create extraordinary results. It had enabled me to take my first step when the doctors had said I would never walk again. It had worked when I had been attempting to break sales records. It had proven effective and reliable for every single person I had ever taught it to. It is the formula that had worked throughout history for some of the world's most prolific achievers. So the first thing I did was summon my Unwavering Faith to clear my head of fear.

Now, I didn't go to the extreme of thinking that I could just sit back and passively maintain faith that I would land in the minority 30 percent of ALL patients who beat their disease and live. In an attempt to turn that 30 percent into 100 percent, I acknowledged my fear and then made a conscious choice to maintain Unwavering Faith that I would live a long, healthy life, no matter what . . . there was no other option. I also made a commitment to myself that I would put forth Extraordinary Effort and do whatever I had to do to stay alive. I used Unwavering Faith to focus on the possibilities in front of me, which included more than just dying. I decided that I was not going to let the statistics confine me. Not only was I committed to beating this cancer, but I decided that I was committed to live to be a hundred years old. I started visualizing celebrating my one hundredth birthday with my family, when my daughter (who was in first grade) will be seventy and my son (who was in preschool) will be sixty-seven. In my mind, there was simply *no other option*. Figuring out the process to get there, though, was not so straightforward.

One of my major challenges was the decision whether or not to do the doctor's recommended treatment: hyper-CVAD chemotherapy. I'm about as "all natural" as it gets. The idea of putting chemotherapy drugs into my body, which are highly toxic poisons aimed at killing the cancer before they kill the person, violated just about every health-related philosophy that I live by.

Second, hyper-CVAD chemotherapy is one of the most intense chemotherapy regimens in existence. Though chemotherapy drugs and regimens vary, many cancer patients' regimens involve going into a hospital or clinic once or twice a month for an hour or two. That alone makes most folks pretty sick from the side effects.

Hyper-CVAD, on the other hand, consists of two combinations of four to five chemotherapy drugs (courses A and B) given in an alternating fashion, each over a four- to five-day period, totaling more than 650 hours of inpatient chemotherapy treatment. The chemotherapy is so toxic that it would permanently damage my veins and had to be administered via a PICC line—a tube installed in my arm that ran through my vein and dispersed the chemo drugs into my more durable artery. Hyper-CVAD chemo must be given in smaller doses to minimize side effects. And there are serious life-threatening side effects and complications arising from the administration of the various drugs, which require careful oversight by medical professionals inside a hospital. In fact, imagine my despair when I learned that one of the many life-threatening side effects listed for one of the drugs I was supposed to take is leukemia. *What?* The so-called medicine that would be injected into my veins to treat my acute lymphoblastic leukemia *causes* leukemia?

The goal was to administer as many cycles as possible (or necessary) in as short a time as possible, in an attempt to kill the cancer before it killed me. Doctors told me that the timing of each cycle would be somewhat dependent on how well my body recovered from the prior cycle. In other words, the amount of damage the chemo did to my body would determine how soon I could take more of it.

If chemotherapy wreaks havoc on your body—and all chemotherapy does—this chemotherapy wreaks the most havoc on your body. People actually die from this treatment, not the cancer. It's kind of crazy to think that you're taking a medicine to save your life but it's killing you in the process. The hope is that the treatment will kill the cancer first and that the person's body will be strong enough to live through the period of killing the cancer before he or she dies.

I'm sure you can imagine how mentally challenging that decision was for me. The regimen was life-threatening in itself. Would I die from the treatment that we were all hoping would save my life? On top of that, I was such a firm believer in not introducing anything toxic into my system. It just went against my whole way of being. I couldn't help but think, *There has to be a better way.*

I was quickly assigned to one of the top leukemia oncologists in the world, Dr. Elias Jabbour at MD Anderson Cancer Center. At our first meeting in his office, I sat next to my wife, Ursula, feeling lost and afraid. Holding hands, we expressed our concerns and asked Dr. Jabbour if he would support me in healing my cancer naturally.

His response caught me off guard. He told me that although he appreciated that I wanted to heal my cancer naturally, ALL was not a cancer that would afford me that option. He explained that I didn't have a slow-growing tumor and pointed out that I had been healthy the week before and now my lungs, heart, and kidneys were on the verge of failing. He assured me that if hyper-CVAD chemotherapy wasn't administered quickly, I would be dead in a few days, maybe a week at most. Ursula broke down crying. She squeezed my hand so hard that I actually winced.

Although I didn't like my oncologist's answer for obvious reasons, it also made me question his motives. I had just met the man, so I didn't know his heart. *Was this a scare tactic?* I wondered. My inner skeptic charged forward. I asked if we could have twenty-four hours to discuss our options. Dr. Jabbour agreed, albeit reluctantly.

That night, Ursula and I scoured the pages of Google in an attempt to gain some clarity. I was desperately searching for evidence that we could approach this holistically. But there was none. In fact, everything we read only confirmed that Dr. Jabbour was being completely honest. If I didn't start chemo immediately, I would have very little chance of surviving. And if I did start it, my odds of surviving were somewhere between 10 and 30 percent.

In a last-ditch effort, I woke up the next morning and placed a call to the office of one of the top holistic cancer doctors in the world, who happened to be located in Houston. He had worked with and cured thousands of cancer patients, including celebrities such as Suzanne Somers. I was hopeful.

When I told his nurse over the phone that I had acute lymphoblastic leukemia with an NUP1 mutation, she put me on hold so that she could relay my diagnosis to the doctor. When she returned to the phone a minute later, she told me that she was sorry, but he had no experience treating that particular type of cancer and wouldn't be able to help me.

You can imagine what I was thinking: *If one of the best holistic cancer doctors in the world isn't able to help me, and everything I've read says that this cancer will kill me in a matter of days if I don't start hyper-CVAD chemotherapy, but one of the side effects of hyper-CVAD is that it may cause leukemia, what am I supposed to do?* There were no clear answers. Lying in a hotel room 170 miles away from our home and our two kids, Ursula and I made the difficult decision for me to start hyper-CVAD chemotherapy. I made a phone call to Dr. Jabbour's office, and an hour later, I was sitting in a hospital bed as a PICC line was installed into my arm.

While countless prayers were to come, the initial ones were from a place of genuine curiosity: *God, I already died once; why is this happening to me? What else can I possibly learn from another major adversity?* As I would come to find out, *a lot.*

## UNWAVERING FAITH FEEDS EXTRAORDINARY EFFORT

During the next twelve months, I spent my time living between three locations: the hospital at MD Anderson Cancer Center, a neighboring apartment that I rented so that I could recover after my treatments, and occasional trips home to be with my family. Speaking of family, my care was truly a family effort. My dad, a successful executive, put his career on hold and dropped everything to move in with me and be my primary caretaker. He took me to my appointments, sat with me while I was given chemo, and rushed me to the ER every time my temperature spiked (infections can be fatal when you are getting chemo because your immune system becomes so compromised). My mom and sister made many trips across the country and stayed with me in the hospital, or babysat my kids so that my wife could stay with me. While all of this was going on in and around the hospital, Ursula—my rock—had, in my opinion, the most difficult job of all. She was balancing between driving to Houston to stay with me during my treatments and trying to create a sense of normalcy for our kids back at home in Austin, 170 miles away. Literally overnight she went from having me at home to help raise our kids to her essentially becoming a single parent, coupled with the stress and fear of losing me. There are no words to express my gratitude for my family, and Ursula most of all.

What allowed me to maintain my sanity during this difficult time was my decision to maintain Unwavering Faith. Consider that the first thing that goes out the window when you're given a statistic like the one I had been given, when the odds are stacked against you, is faith. We must consciously decide to maintain Unwavering Faith despite the statistics or the odds we're faced with. Making and maintaining that decision removes you from those statistics and places you in the minority of people who consistently defy the odds. Contrary to what many people think, maintaining faith isn't limited to blindly following the beliefs and teachings of others. Rather, it is having faith in yourself and your commitment to put forth Extraordinary Effort to do whatever it takes to generate your ideal outcome.

That's where my holistic measures came in. In addition to receiving the most advanced medical care from Dr. Jabbour and MD Anderson Cancer Center, I immediately went on a quest to find the most effective and proven methods of holistic treatment—detoxifying my body (from the chemo), boosting my immune system, and creating an environment in which cancer cannot thrive. This included eating a primarily plant-based diet, drinking fresh organic vegetable juices, and ingesting upward of seventy natural supplements each day. I also engaged in weekly acupuncture and ozone sauna sessions, did coffee enemas, used a device called a BEMER mat twice a day, took CBD oil, meditated, prayed, exercised, recited cancer-related affirmations, and much more. The research I did, combined with the holistic practices that resulted, became my Extraordinary Effort.

## UNWAVERING FAITH IN ACTION

A while back, when I was toying with the idea of this book, I wrote to the Miracle Morning Community (Facebook group) asking if anyone had a Miracle Equation story he or she could share. I received many inspiring stories, including this one. I was especially taken with this story because it had so many similarities to my own cancer journey. It just goes to show that the equation really does work for everyone who applies it.

Rachel Harris first learned about the Miracle Equation when she was diagnosed with cancer. At the age of thirty-eight, her bowel cancer had spread to her liver and lymph nodes, and doctors told her that her cancer was inoperable. She was put on palliative chemotherapy. As a mother of two young children, she refused to accept the prognosis and committed to applying the Miracle Equation to her life. According to Rachel, "We live and breathe the Equation."

Here is where the miracle comes in. Despite the doctors' grim forecast, after one round of chemo, her tumors shrank and were suddenly operable. Rachel continued to combine her Unwavering Faith that she would live a long and happy life with Extraordinary Effort, making significant changes to her diet, taking a bunch of supplements, meditating every morning, staying fit, and doing as much research as she could on how to heal her body. She also said, "The Miracle Equation has set the tone of my cancer journey and I will always live by it. I think it may well have saved my life!"

After enduring the most difficult, painful, and gut-wrenching year of my life—including more than 650 hours of chemotherapy and spending many nights in the ER fighting for my life—I am beyond grateful to tell you that I recently received a new diagnosis: I am "in remission from cancer." This means that doctors are unable to detect any cancer in my body. Yes, I had to endure some painful side effects. Yes, I feared dying and leaving my wife and kids. And yes, there were many days when I doubted myself and was tempted to give up. But I believe that I was able to handle all of it so much better than most people do because I actively maintained Unwavering Faith every step of the way. Even my doctors were a bit shocked at how positive and upbeat I remained, even during the worst of my treatments.

Most important, I survived and am now able to follow through with my commitment to live a long, healthy life with my family.

## WHERE TO FIND YOUR UNWAVERING FAITH

In my most recent experience of using the Miracle Equation to create a tangible, measurable miracle (overcoming cancer), it's fair to say that I had an advantage since I had used the equation many times in the past. And I had watched other people use it. I understand how it works—and, more important, *that* it works. And so I was able to stick with it. I could tap into the Unwavering Faith within. But if you're not there yet, don't worry. There are plenty of places from which you can borrow it.

If you've seen *The Miracle Morning* documentary, you know the story of Rister Ratemo. When Rister started losing her eyesight at age fourteen, she maintained Unwavering Faith that God would heal her eyes and restore her vision. She then used her faith to feed her Extraordinary Effort and fly herself halfway around the world, from her home in Kenya to a clinic in the United States, to have her first of six surgeries. Part of what made her effort extraordinary is that Rister had no choice but to make the trip alone, while nearly blind, because in the Kenyan culture, it is taboo to take another person's body part, and the operation involved a corneal transplant. Rister found her faith in God and religion. If you find comfort in religion or spirituality, tapping into those resources can help you to maintain your Unwavering Faith.

Religion and spirituality are one source of externally based Unwavering Faith. But there are plenty more. Often a coach or a mentor is a good source of Unwavering Faith. I liken this idea to the movie *The Matrix*. Remember how Laurence Fishburne's character, Morpheus, kept telling Keanu Reeves's character, Neo, that he was "the one"? It wasn't until Neo, too, believed that he was indeed the one that he gained full access to all of his potential. Similarly, when you believe that you are the one—the one who is just as deserving, worthy, and capable as any other person on Earth—you will gain full access to your limitless potential.

In the same light, before I had faith in myself, I borrowed it from my first manager at Cutco, Jesse Levine (the same Jesse who taught me the Five-Minute Rule). Jesse had faith in my ability to break various sales records in the Cutco Corporation. From the first day we met, he believed that I could accomplish things that had never been accomplished before.

At first, though it felt good to hear him say those things, I didn't believe he was right. A lifetime of insecurities and self-doubt had left me fighting an internal battle with my own limitless potential. *Jesse thinks I'm capable of anything, but he doesn't really know that deep down, I'm terrified of failing.* But eventually, through Jesse's unwavering faith in me, I started to consider that what he was saying could be true. *Maybe I really am capable of accomplishing anything I put my mind to.* Eventually Jesse's faith in me became my faith in myself, and that was when I claimed my inherent power to create an extraordinary life. Sometimes you have to borrow the faith that someone else has in you until your faith in yourself catches up.

If you're at all concerned because you don't have a mentor readily available, rest assured because you can also borrow Unwavering Faith from a complete stranger. I'm referring to someone you've studied or witnessed from afar. Maybe it's an athlete who just won the world championship, or an Olympian, such as Michael Phelps, who won many gold medals. Maybe it's a CEO or a self-made millionaire who has achieved results that you aspire to achieve yourself. You can read their books, track their progress, or listen to their interviews with the press to study their mindset and catch glimpses into the way they think:

"I've visualized this moment thousands of times."

"There was no doubt in my mind that we would win."

"I've worked too hard not to be the best."

In doing so, you will realize that behind the scenes, when no one is looking, these champions—these Miracle Mavens—are cultivating Unwavering Faith. That is the mindset that makes them champions. They are always willing to take the next shot, so to speak, because they have faith that they will make it. And if they miss, their faith doesn't waver, because they believe they'll make the next one. They never shy away from opportunities. They run toward them.

I'll never forget Reggie Miller's awe-inspiring comeback against the Knicks, when he used the Miracle Equation to score a seemingly impossible *eight points in nine seconds* in the 1995 NBA Eastern Conference semifinals. It didn't seem possible, and it sure as hell wasn't probable. No player had accomplished such a feat before, and none has since. Reggie is another example of someone who maintained Unwavering Faith and put forth Extraordinary Effort until the last possible moment. He believed he could defy the odds, and he did.

Unwavering Faith will always unlock the potential that has been lying dormant within you and open up new possibilities that once seemed out of reach.

If you struggle to find others who embody Unwavering Faith, consider borrowing it from the authors of the books you read. (Of course, you can start with this one.) I consider the author of every book I read to be a mentor. Even though we're not face to face, I'm still learning from him or her.

You can always fall back on the universal truism that if another human being has done something that you desire, their accomplishment serves as evidence that it's also possible for you. If the world's top performers, in all walks of life, consciously choose to live from a place of Unwavering Faith, you can make that same conscious choice. And you can start now.

## ONE TOOL FOR MAINTAINING UNWAVERING FAITH

Once you make the decision to view your goals through the lens of Unwavering Faith, you need to maintain it, which is easier said than done. Even small obstacles can throw you off track. You don't need to be faced with a life-or-death situation to feel as though your hope is slipping away. The self-doubt we all deal with is reinforced each time we encounter a roadblock along the way. In my case, every time I got sick from chemo, I felt weak and was tempted to give up. But I didn't.

The tool I have always used to keep me focused on my Unwavering Faith in my goal and myself is what I call my *Miracle Mantra*. You may remember when I introduced it in chapter 2: *I am committed to maintaining Unwavering Faith that I will sell $20,000 for push, and I will continue putting forth Extraordinary Effort until I do, no matter what . . . there is no other option.* That single sentence kept me moving forward when I wasn't on track and was tempted to give up, and it can do the same for you. Your Miracle Mantra is a single sentence that encapsulates your commitment to your mission and reminds you that maintaining Unwavering Faith and putting forth Extraordinary Effort—over an extended period of time—are what will make your miracle a reality.

When I was going through cancer treatment, I repeated the following Miracle Mantra countless times: *I am committed to maintaining Unwavering Faith that I will beat cancer and live a long, healthy life with my family, and I will continue putting forth Extraordinary Effort until I do, no matter what . . . there is no other option.* By repeating this, I strengthened my inner resolve to keep fighting, to continue putting forth Extraordinary Effort, especially when I felt like giving up.

Here is the basic template to create your Miracle Mantra: *I am committed to maintaining Unwavering Faith that I will _____ [insert your mission], and I will continue putting forth Extraordinary Effort until I do. No matter what, there is no other option.*

**Take some time now to write down your first Miracle Mantra.**

_____

_____

_____

_____

Your Miracle Mantra is your guiding compass. Your North Star. Your reminder. It keeps you focused on what you've committed to and overrides the unyielding voice of self-doubt. Think of it as a megaphone for your integrity. It keeps your mission front and center and serves as your constant reminder: *I am fully committed, no matter what . . . there is no other option.*

Now that you know how to establish and maintain the mindset of a Miracle Maven, the next chapter will explore the second half of the Miracle Equation, Extraordinary Effort. We'll explore what it takes to move from having faith that your miracle is possible to turning it into a tangible reality.

8

# YOUR SECOND DECISION: EXTRAORDINARY EFFORT

It's Less Extraordinary

Than You Think

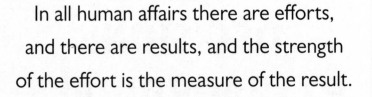

In all human affairs there are efforts,
and there are results, and the strength
of the effort is the measure of the result.

—JAMES ALLEN

don't know about you, but I've always considered myself to be a pretty lazy person. As I was growing up, the idea of working hard wasn't appealing, so I avoided anything that involved "hard work." I vividly recall that after any holiday get-together with my extended family, when everyone else was cleaning up our cocreated mess, I would disappear and hide in my bedroom until everyone else took care of it. If there was anything that required even ordinary effort, I was nowhere to be found.

It didn't matter what the activity was, from schoolwork to chores to my first few jobs during grade school, I developed the habit of putting forth the minimum amount of effort necessary to keep from suffering any significant negative consequences, such as being grounded or getting fired. Being lazy became a deeply ingrained part of my identity.

As I got older, I figured out tricks and shortcuts that would make it relatively easy to do the work I had to do, so that it never felt like hard work. Either I would make a game out of it, distract myself by multitasking, or delegate the job to my little sister. Sometimes I could muster up enough internal fortitude to tackle a larger project, but I could never sustain my short-lived work sprints long enough to see myself as a disciplined person. And that was my biggest challenge: I couldn't figure out how to see myself as any better than I had been in my past.

Even when I put in a sixty-plus-hour workweek to break a sales record (at age nineteen), woke up every day at 3:30 a.m. to write *The Miracle Morning* (at age twenty-eight), or ran twenty-plus miles per week to train for my first (and last) ultramarathon (at age thirty), my distorted self-image was still that of a lazy individual who had managed to trick himself into working hard for only a small window of time. No matter what I did, I still saw myself as the same lazy kid that I had been my entire life. This is *potential dysmorphia* in its truest form. After my short bursts of activity, I'd fall back into my old pattern of putting forth the minimal amount of effort necessary to avoid suffering any negative consequences, much as I did as a child. The only thing that was consistent was my inconsistency.

However, and surprisingly, there was and still is tremendous value in such shortcuts and self-trickery—because I figured out how, even as a lazy person, I could get myself to achieve significant results and reach levels of success that I had never imagined to be possible, at least not for me. Over time, the more and more I was able to trick myself into working hard, albeit for short periods of time, the more my identity began to change from that of a lazy person to that of a disciplined individual. Slowly but surely, as I gradually improved my identity, I saw improvements in both my results and my consistency.

So how does a self-proclaimed lazy person transform into a self-disciplined, hardworking individual who is capable of consistently putting forth Extraordinary Effort and creating miracles? By simplifying Extraordinary Effort so that it feels much less . . . extraordinary.

In this chapter, I'm going to simplify what it means to give Extraordinary Effort to everything that we do and show you exactly how to get yourself to take action, consistently and even when you don't feel like it, so that you can put the Miracle Equation to work and start experiencing miracles in all areas of your life.

## MAKING EXTRAORDINARY EFFORT ORDINARY

As we've discussed, Extraordinary Effort is the second decision you must make to implement the Miracle Equation. Once you believe that it's not only possible but possible for you, you have to take the necessary actions that will make your success inevitable. Creating miracles requires active engagement—and sustained effort. You must be willing to put in the time and effort it takes to create meaningful results, which will transform how you see yourself. But before you close this book, let me also explain that putting forth Extraordinary Effort doesn't mean that you are going to work yourself to the bone and risk burning yourself out. Actually, it's quite the contrary.

Extraordinary Effort has three components:

- ✓ Actions that move you closer to your ideal results
- ✓ Actions that will most likely take you out of your comfort zone
- ✓ Consistent effort over an extended period of time (regardless of your results along the way)

That doesn't seem horrible, right? Now let's look at each of these three components separately.

**Actions that move you closer to your ideal results** ensure that you don't run yourself ragged wasting time on tasks and activities that will yield only short-term benefits or have minimal impact, serving a purpose no greater than simply keeping you busy and distracted from what really matters. This means that you must keep your mind focused and your actions productive. Instead of wearing you down, the actions you take should energize you. They should be measurable. And they should be meaningful. More on that throughout this chapter.

**Actions that will most likely move you out of your comfort zone** are where your growth lies. You are never going to become a Miracle Maven doing the exact same things you've always done. Getting out of your comfort zone always feels unnerving at first, but over time it will become your new norm, your new productivity and effort set point.

**Consistent effort over an extended period of time (regardless of your results along the way)** is the glue that holds all of this together. You aren't going to get anywhere if you take only a few steps and then quit. You must remain committed for an extended period of time to go the distance. The flip side of this is that consistency makes things easier. Remember how you need to move out of your comfort zone? Well, after you've been out of your comfort zone for a few weeks, it no longer feels so uncomfortable. As you expand your comfort zone, you also expand what's possible for you.

David Osborn, a *New York Times* bestselling coauthor of *Wealth Can't Wait: Avoid the 7 Wealth Traps, Implement the 7 Business Pillars, and Complete a Life Audit Today!* and a coauthor of *Miracle Morning Millionaires: What the Wealthy Do Before 8AM That Will Make You Rich*, often talks about how becoming wealthy is simply a choice. If you make the choice to study wealthy individuals, adopt their mindset (faith), and model their behavior (effort) over a sustained period of time, you will experience similar results. Of course, you can replace "becoming wealthy" with any desired result that's important to you (being happy, being healthy, being a great parent, and so on).

If you believe that's true, and I do believe that it is for most people, why isn't everyone wealthy? Because creating extraordinary wealth requires Extraordinary Effort, and it's easier to keep doing what we're already doing than it is to do anything else. Whether or not you consider yourself to be hardworking and disciplined, most of us would rather put forth as little effort as possible to generate our desired outcomes. And that's fine, as long as you can figure out which effort(s) will ensure that you generate your desired outcomes.

Let's break down how you're going to map out which efforts will ensure that you generate your desired outcomes *and* make Extraordinary Effort ordinary.

### STEP I: Predetermine your process.

Once you have settled on your singular mission with the primary objective of evolving into a more capable version of yourself and made the decision to maintain Unwavering Faith that you will achieve it, you must determine what your process will be. Every goal or result that we wish to achieve is preceded and created by a process—the specific actions necessary to produce the desired results and ultimately the life that those results will create for us.

Which tasks will you perform every day, before anything else? If you're not sure what those tasks should be, do some research. Search on Google for steps to achieve the type of goal you're working toward, or search Amazon for bestselling books in your category. Reach out to a mentor or another Miracle Maven. It's okay if the first step in your process is to research and figure out what your process should be.

When I decided to hit the $200,000 sales mark while working at Cutco, the first thing I did was call my colleagues who had already achieved that goal. I had a list of written questions about the mental and emotional aspects of achieving such a lofty goal, as well as what they did from day to day and from week to week, to make it happen. I wanted to understand their process for achieving that level of success.

Once I had interviewed all of them, I realized that they all had one thing in common: *consistency*. They weren't doing any specific activities that were different from what I was doing. They didn't possess any special talents or sales tricks. They were simply committed to the process of making a predetermined number of phone calls and scheduling a predetermined number of appointments to be in line with their sales goals. All reps do that. What set the high achievers apart was that they consistently made that predetermined number of calls every day and went on a predetermined number of appointments every week, without fail. Whereas I would work in sprints and earn enough money to take some time off and enjoy the fruits of my labor, those folks stayed the course, executing their predetermined process every day, no matter what. The saying "Successful people make a habit of doing what unsuccessful people do only some of the time" suddenly made a lot of sense.

After I uncovered the not-so-glamorous secret of their success, the rest was just going through the motions. I predetermined my process by calculating how many appointments I needed to schedule in order to reach my sales goal and then translated that number into how many calls that would require. I determined that to sell more than $200,000 of Cutco for the year, all I would have to do was consistently make a minimum of two hundred calls every week (forty calls a day times five days a week) in order to schedule an average of fourteen appointments, which would result in an average of ten sales for approximately $4,000 per week.

Forty calls a day didn't feel extraordinary. I had made forty calls in a single day plenty of times. I had just never *consistently* made that number of calls. In fact, in the two years in which I had surpassed the $100,000 mark, not surprisingly, I had averaged just over twenty calls a day, five days a week. So it wasn't rocket science: double my calls, double my sales, double my income. Making forty sales calls took me about two hours, and then the rest was just showing up to the appointments I had scheduled. Suddenly that intimidating goal, one that had terrified me and had been achieved by less than a handful of sales reps in the fifty-plus-year history of the company, seemed almost too easy. This is the power of predetermining your process and making your Extraordinary Effort feel ordinary. Often our major goals are big and scary, but the process almost never is. Some other examples include the following:

Shedding unwanted pounds will always be preceded by a process that consists of exercising and managing your caloric intake (and maybe figuring out what foods work best for your body and when).

If you want to become financially free, you can get there only by committing to a process that consists of earning and saving significantly more money than the amount that you need to pay your bills.

If you want to run a marathon, surpassing 26.2 miles on run day must be preceded by a process of training, usually running a specific number of miles per day or per week in the lead-up to the marathon.

If you want to publish a book, you will need to commit to a process of writing consistently. In order to complete this book, I've committed to writing 1,000 words every single day whether I feel like it or not (and trust me, I don't always feel like it).

As you can see, your process does not have to be some intricate and complicated plan; the simpler, the better. All you have to do is decide what the process is that will keep you on track with achieving your mission, commit to the process, and put it into your schedule. That's it; nothing more and nothing less. As soon as you've completed your predetermined tasks for the day, the ones that will make achieving your mission inevitable, you are free to move on to making progress on your other goals.

To predetermine your process, simply ask yourself: *Which activities, done consistently, will make my success inevitable?*

## STEP 2: Release any emotional attachment to your results.

With regard to our process, the one thing that is certain is that there will be bad days. There might even be bad weeks. But knowing they are inevitable doesn't make them any more palatable. The fact is that human beings are emotional creatures. As emotional creatures, we are emotionally attached to our results, but our emotional attachment hinders our ability to remain committed to the process that will put us on the path to achieve those results. For most people, not accomplishing what they set out to is frustrating, draining, and discouraging. But it doesn't have to be. When you commit to your process and release your emotional attachment to your day-to-day results, your long-term results will inevitably take care of themselves without you needing to get frustrated along the way.

Here are a few examples of how this has played out in real life:

1.  I have a friend whose goal was to lose weight. He defined his process, based on limiting his caloric intake, eating a primarily plant-based diet, and exercising regularly. One day he called me and said, "Hal, I'm trying your prede-

termined process strategy. For the past three weeks, I've been exercising four days a week for thirty minutes each day, but I haven't lost any weight. In fact, I gained a pound, and I don't understand why. I'm feeling demotivated." I told him to check his body fat percentage because there was a good chance that he had gained muscle, which would offset his weight loss. Sure enough, that's what had happened. After three months, his body fat percentage dropped from 24 percent to 14 percent. And that's because he remained committed to his process every day. Had he given up when he didn't see the scale responding as he had hoped, he wouldn't be as fit and healthy as he is today.

2. I also had a client years ago who managed one of the top sales teams in the country within his company. He was a superstar who was used to getting great results. His goal during our time working together was to lead his sales team to $1.3 million in sales for the year. The one coaching call that stands out most to me was when he was down and scared because his team's sales had slumped in the few weeks leading up to our call. He kept coming back to his annual business plan, and specifically the weekly sales projections that he had forecast at the beginning of the year. He was having trouble understanding why, despite doing everything he was supposed to do, his reps' results were not meeting his sales projections.

   I pointed out to him that his emotional attachment to his team's short-term, day-to-day results could cause his commitment to his process to waver, because he wasn't in control of his reps' day-to-day results, at least not directly. Sure, he could *influence* their results, but he couldn't *control* them. He couldn't control how many people answered the phone when his reps called or their prospects' moods when they answered the phone. He couldn't control who did or didn't schedule an appointment with individual members of his sales team or who showed up for the appointments they had scheduled. He couldn't control who bought from his reps, gave them referrals, and so on. Yet his emotions were attached to all of those results and many more. Once he realized that all he had to do was ensure that his reps made their phone calls—the only thing that he (or they) could control—his whole job changed for him. He no longer allowed his mood and motivation to be influenced by his reps' short-term results. Once he made that decision, he let go of how much his team sold on any given day and even whether or not they reached their sales goal for the week. He accepted whatever the results were going to be before they even happened (remember our "Can't change it" conversation?). He remained focused on the big picture and had faith that if he continued to implement his own process, which was to ensure that his reps completed their sales calls for the day over a sustained period of time, the results would always average out. I actually felt his stress melt away over the course of that call as he realized that he had to focus only on his own process.

3. I'll give you one more personal example. When *The Miracle Morning* was published, I had very few resources beyond what the average person would have to promote the book. I didn't have a platform or a big email list. And I didn't know anyone else who did. So I asked myself what the best

way to promote my new book would be. After speaking to a lot of authors and doing online research, I decided that the fundamental strategy I was going to implement was being interviewed on podcasts. I surmised that the type of person who listens to podcast interviews is the same type of person who invests in personal development. It's also a very cost-effective strategy, since being interviewed on a podcast costs nothing other than your time.

I have since done more than three hundred podcast interviews plus produced more than two hundred of my own *Achieve Your Goals* podcast episodes. It took me eighteen months of interviews just to sell again what I had sold in the first month after the book was released. The graph below shows the value of remaining committed to your process *for an extended period of time,* regardless of your short-term results. That was eighteen months in which I saw very few sales in proportion to the amount

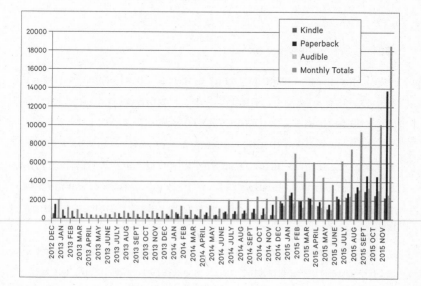

of time and effort I was investing in securing and conducting podcast interviews. As you can see by looking at the graph on the previous page, I didn't sell many books from December 2012 through June 2014, which means my effort wasn't paying dividends in the short term. Had I been emotionally attached to my short-term results, I never would have made it. But I believed in the book and knew that it would change people's lives, so I stuck to my process and remained focused on the big picture. Ultimately, my commitment to my process paid off. As of today, *The Miracle Morning* has surpassed over one million copies sold, half of them here in the United States and the other half spread across more than a hundred countries around the world—further evidence that although achieving significant goals often takes longer than we might want or expect, when we maintain Unwavering Faith and continue to put forth Extraordinary Effort over an extended period of time, we can create miracles.

**STEP 3:** Schedule your process.

We all know what it feels like to buy new gym clothes or order a bunch of books on a topic you are interested in learning about—and then to watch them sit in the corner of your room unused. We get busy. The kids get sick. A client throws some more work on us. Life happens.

One way to help ensure that you follow through with your process is to schedule it, ideally as a recurring appointment. You must be proactive with your days and how you spend your time, or nothing will change.

Take out your calendar, physical or digital, and write or type in when you will complete your process each day and specifically what the process entails. If you are working toward getting a postgraduate degree, you may commit to how many classes you will take each semester as well as block out times for studying and doing homework. If you use a digital calendar (which I highly recommend), make it a recurring appointment. Then all you have to do is show up. If you want to spend more time with your kids, schedule that time into your calendar. If your goal is to create more free time for yourself, schedule that, too. Most important, don't let anything interfere with this time. Protect the time you need to complete your process and achieve your mission above all else. This is how you ensure that your mission will move from possible to probable to what we're all after: making the attainment of your mission inevitable.

I realize that this may sound a bit overboard, as though I'm holding your hand too much. But I've found that if something isn't important enough to make it onto your schedule, chances are it's not going to happen. At least not consistently.

If you feel as though you might be overwhelmed by adding more to your already packed plate, go ahead and evaluate your schedule for the rest of your day. Look at where you can be more efficient, or replace low-priority activities with those that are mission critical and will get you where you want to go. Maybe you can have your errands done for you by taking advantage of one of the many relatively inexpensive delivery services (most of which are available as apps on your smart phone), such as Instacart, Amazon Prime Now, or one of the many food delivery services, including Uber Eats, Favor, Grubhub, and DoorDash. I use all of these services (and more) so that I can focus more of my time on what matters most, my mission and other goals. Or you might give up an hour of watching television to play with your kids. Or you can wake up an hour earlier in order to work on launching your new business. It's easier to get where you want to go when you're not only clear about exactly which actions will get you there and when you will do them, but also when they're written in your schedule.

## STEP 4: Safeguard your success with accountability.

You know yourself better than anyone else does. So what do you think it will take for you to commit—and stay committed—to your process? Are you someone who is fairly self-reliant, and once you commit to something, you follow through whether someone else is holding you accountable or not? If so, you'll do fine implementing the Miracle Equation on your own. Many people, though, get excited in the beginning and then fade off somewhere around the middle.

The fact is, it's not easy to stick with anything for the extended amount of time necessary to produce a meaningful outcome. If it was, everyone would do it and there would be no need for this book. However, self-discipline isn't so common. If we could all go it alone, everyone would be achieving all of their goals all of the time. I know we discussed this in chapter 6, but it's worth repeating: one of the best ways to ensure that you follow through is by establishing some peer-to-peer accountability. It'll keep you honest, and it'll keep you moving forward.

Accountability is the condition of being responsible to someone or something or responsible for some action or result, and it can come in a variety of shapes and sizes. Some people function best with a deadline. Others respond to the avoidance of negative consequences, and yet others work best with rewards. It's important for you to figure out what motivates you most and then put it into action. Oftentimes, asking someone else to hold you accountable is key, and providing mutual accountability is even better.

Reaching out to someone else to help you with your goal isn't weak, nor does it make you ineffective. It makes you smart. Show me a

Fortune 500 CEO who isn't supported with an extraordinary amount of accountability. He or she has to answer to shareholders, staff members, the company's executive board, and often an executive coach. Asking someone else (or a group of people) to hold you accountable anchors your commitment. Think about it: Isn't it easier to make it to the gym when you have a trainer there waiting for you? And isn't it easier to tackle a long run when you're running with a friend? Whatever your goal may be, you can find an accountability partner, ask a mentor for check-ins, build your own accountability team (there's no better way to hold yourself accountable to do something than when you have to lead others to do the same), or hire a coach to help you get there. Remember, though, that in order to get the most out of your accountability source, the other person or people must be rigid, must be consistent, and must care about you and your success.

**STEP 5**: Assess your results and adjust your process accordingly.

As you follow through with your process, it is important that you pay attention to how your results are going. If, after two months, the scale hasn't budged, you may need to reassess your meal plan or exercise. If you're not hitting your sales goal, an increase in prospecting or marketing activities may be in order. If you haven't written anything for your book idea, go back to your schedule and see if you can move your writing time.

I recommend scheduling weekly or monthly check-ins with yourself to see if your process warrants tweaking based on your results so far. The goal is always to make your process as clear and as easy as possible, so you'll follow through with it. If there is anything getting in the way of that, these check-ins are a great time to make changes.

## YOU'VE ACHIEVED YOUR MIRACLE. NOW WHAT?

Remember, the Miracle Equation isn't about attaining one miracle and then going back to the way things were. We want to join the ranks of the Miracle Mavens, who create tangible, measurable miracles over and over again in all areas of life. To do this, it's imperative that the more successes you have, the more you continue to elevate and evolve your goals.

Extract and internalize the lessons you learn along the way and use them to propel you into your next mission. As I mentioned earlier, I established a mission to spend more time with my family. Once that was on autopilot, I established a mission to remain cancer-free, for the rest of my life. Once that was on autopilot, I turned my attention to the mission of writing this book. Each mission you commit to will further develop your capabilities as a Miracle Maven, and no miracle will be out of reach for you.

### YOUR PROCESS IN ACTION

My favorite musician in the world is a man named Jeremy Reisig, otherwise known as "brotha James." He is a uniquely talented musician who brings a lot of positivity into the world through his songs. His music is designed to make you feel good. In fact, he is the only musician that I'm aware of who combines positive affirmations with upbeat music, so that every lyric you hear programs your subconscious mind for greater happiness and success.

At the start of his music career, Jeremy toured with a funk band. He played several instruments and rapped, but he also wanted to sing backup vocals. Time and again, the band members turned him down because they said his voice just wasn't good enough.

So in 2013, after four years with the band, he decided he was going to learn how to sing and become a songwriter. He wanted to live his dream to be the lead singer of a band. He asked a few people to join him, but they, too, didn't think that his voice was strong enough. Ouch.

With an unwavering commitment to making his dream a reality, he began taking singing lessons with two different vocal instructors. He practiced nearly every single day for fifteen to thirty minutes and kept his faith that he would one day reach his goal. Keep in mind that his Extraordinary Effort was merely practicing for fifteen to thirty minutes each day. That feels pretty ordinary. What made it extraordinary was his commitment and consistency over an extended period of time, until he got his first gig in March 2014. Then his efforts really paid off when he finally got his first *paid* gig in the middle of 2015.

Today, brotha James travels the country living his dream as an inspirational musician. He continues to take classes and still fulfills his commitment of practicing fifteen to thirty minutes five days a week. In his words, "The micro done over and over again creates the macro." His commitment to the process continues to pay off. His voice has gone from bad to good to excellent, as he's regularly compared to the famed singer Jason Mraz. Jeremy continues to improve and bring his music to more and more people. Last year, brotha James did more than 150 different types of musical engagements. He is the perfect example of how committing to a process over time makes success inevitable.

## HOW TO GET YOURSELF TO DO THE THINGS YOU KNOW YOU SHOULD BE DOING (EVEN WHEN YOU DON'T FEEL LIKE DOING THEM)

A very common question that I get from clients and readers alike is "How do I motivate myself to do the things that I know I should do?" Their underlying tone is usually one of frustration or helplessness.

Ever since we were kids, doing what we should do has never come easily. As much as we know that eating more vegetables will make us healthier, living below our means is prudent, and taking time during the day to slow down and rest our mind will lower our stress, we often drag our feet or just disregard these things altogether. When it comes to pursuing a meaningful goal, we also have to find a way to overcome the temptation to procrastinate because really, those who do only what they feel like doing . . . don't do much.

Procrastination becomes a way of life, in which we habitually delay doing the activities that are uncomfortable, unproven, or unknown. The same activities that are necessary to moving us from where we are to where we want to be. So how can we get ourselves to do what we know we should do, even when we don't feel like it? By understanding the fundamental cause of procrastination and then doing something to overcome it. I'm sure you can conjure up all kinds of reasons as to why you believe you procrastinate, but there's really only one: *You associate some level of pain, fear, or discomfort with the activity you're procrastinating about.* That's it.

To overcome procrastination, understand that all of that pain, fear, and discomfort is imagined. It's all in your head. And all of it becomes irrelevant in the midst of your doing the thing you perceive as painful, fearful, or uncomfortable. Sure, thinking about doing it is scary. The more you think about it, the more you procrastinate. But actually doing it? Doing the thing you've been thinking about—the thing you know you need to do—is liberating. It frees you from your fear, it's almost never as painful as you told yourself it was going to be, and soon what you imagined would be uncomfortable is nestled gently inside your comfort zone.

So in order for you to find the motivation you need to do the things you habitually procrastinate on, you must *move*. You must take the first step, and that step, that movement, will generate the motivation you need to keep moving forward. But that first step is on you.

If you find yourself procrastinating about going to the gym, just pack your gym bag and jump into the car at the time you designated to work out. Don't think about it, just get into the car. By simply taking your first baby step toward going to the gym, chances are, you'll likely drive to said gym (the one you've been paying the membership fee on for so many months). And when you pull into the parking lot and slide your car into the first available spot, I'll bet you'll be motivated to grab your gym bag off the passenger seat and head inside—at least a hell of a lot more motivated than when you were at home, sitting on your couch, thinking yourself out of going to the gym. When you walk inside, hear the high-energy music blasting through the speakers, and see all of the people pumping iron and running on treadmills, I'd venture to say that you're going to join them. And when you do, you'll feel proud of yourself. You'll realize that the choice to procrastinate is exactly that, a choice—one that you no longer have to settle for now that you're clear about what was causing it.

Overcoming procrastination is simply a matter of taking the first, seemingly inconsequential, step toward doing what you need to do to achieve your goals. Once you begin to move, you've already beat procrastination. Now it's a matter of continuing to move in the same direction. Do that each day with your predetermined process, and before you know it, your only struggle with procrastination will be trying to remember what it felt like.

See, I told you that Extraordinary Effort isn't all that extraordinary. All you need is a simple and repeatable process that you schedule into your calendar, a fair amount of emotional detachment (in the form of being at peace with your day-to-day results, regardless of what they are), some peer-to-peer accountability, and some tweaking along the way. Your process can be as simple (or as complex) as you need it to be. Remember how far brotha James has come with his singing voice with only fifteen to thirty minutes of practice a day. I earned my first six-figure annual income by making forty phone calls a day, which took me only two hours. You may not believe me now, but soon enough you may even look forward to engaging in your process each day. That huge, scary goal becomes fun to tackle once you realize how to approach it.

Now that you know the steps to applying the Miracle Equation, the next chapter is going to dive into how to keep repeating this process to produce miracles in every aspect of your life, over and over again.

# 9

# MAINTAINING MIRACLES

Create Extraordinary Results
Over and Over and Over Again

Miracles only happen
if you believe in miracles.

—PAULO COELHO

t's one thing to get excited about being able to create tangible, measurable miracles. Who wouldn't get excited when given the keys to unlocking the life of their dreams? Maybe you want financial security or freedom. Perhaps you are ready for a special relationship or to repair the one you're in. Maybe you're in search of meaningful work that fulfills you. Or you want to be healthier, more fit, and experience more physical energy. Or maybe you just want to be happy. All that said, getting excited by the possibility of these life enhancements is quite different from making them inevitable.

If the ultimate goal here is for you to develop and embody the characteristics of a Miracle Maven so that you can maintain the ability to create miracles at will, you must think and act like a Miracle Maven. And you must think and act that way *most of the time*.

You must replace fear-based thinking with faith-based thinking. You must be willing to let go of any limitations that you've carried with you from your past, and see yourself as someone who is just as worthy, deserving, and capable of creating everything you want as any other person on Earth. I know we've mentioned this idea a few times (maybe more than a few times), but now I'm going to help you do that at the intellectual *and* the emotional levels, so that you can both see and feel the new, improved you. This will make it much easier to live in alignment with the person you're committed to becoming and the future you're committed to creating.

Earl Nightingale, known for his inspirational audios and books, said, "We become what we think about." The Buddha stated, "We are what we think. All that we are arises with our thoughts. With our thoughts, we make the world." And I've been reminding you that it is indeed our mindset that is responsible for shaping both our identity and our reality. But how much time do you invest in strategically designing your mindset? In this chapter, we're going to drill down on how to reprogram your mind with the thoughts and behaviors that will keep you in Miracle Maven mode. Fortunately, there is one specific practice that works perfectly for this.

## THE SINGLE PRACTICE YOU NEED TO IMPLEMENT THE MIRACLE EQUATION

In my book *The Miracle Morning*, I introduced a framework called the *Life S.A.V.E.R.S.* The acronym represents six of the most timeless, universally applicable, scientifically proven personal development practices in the history of humanity (none of which I invented): Silence, Affirmations, Visualization, Exercise, Reading, and Scribing. I suggest they be done daily, preferably first thing in the morning, to optimize your mindset and focus for the rest of the day.

Though each of these six practices is transformational on its own, I'm often asked, during interviews, if I have a "favorite" of the S.A.V.E.R.S. I'd imagine that the politically correct answer would probably be something like "Of course not; they're all equally important." However, between you and me, I'll always choose to be transparent over politically correct (often to a fault).

So, yes, I do have a favorite, based on what my experience has proven to be most effective. My favorite practice for personal development and transformation is unequivocally the "A" in S.A.V.E.R.S.: Affirmations. But (and this is another big *but*) not in the way that you might think.

You see, affirmations tend to have a bad rap. They're often viewed as ineffective at best or cheesy at worst. They kind of fall into the same bucket as a vision board. If you just post some pictures on your wall and sit back and wait for your reality to magically shift, well, it's probably not going to. Similarly, you can't just talk your way into a new you. Well, you can, but not the way many self-help gurus would have you believe.

When I was younger, I was among the crowd who considered affirmations to be both cheesy *and* ineffective. I thought they were a lot of feel-good statements that had zero grounding in reality and just made people feel better in the moment. People like me, who were results oriented and, you know, sane, didn't bother repeating feel-good statements just to mask our insecurities. I had no confidence that they would actually produce results.

As I entered into my twenties and began studying personal development, I was reintroduced to affirmations as a legitimate tool for transformation. The promise was that I could change my life just by saying certain phrases over and over again until I believed them. For someone who had grown up believing I was lazy and acting accordingly, that sounded right up my alley. *I don't have to do much of anything*, I thought. I was all in.

Until I wasn't. It didn't take long for me to hit the same wall with my affirmations that most people come up against. Nothing happened when I used the format that was commonly taught by pioneers in the self-help field. That great life I kept talking about didn't appear. Repeating "I am a millionaire" over and over again didn't put a dime in my bank account. In fact, using "I am" statements to affirm I was something that I wasn't felt inauthentic.

Then, one day, I had an epiphany. I realized that the flaw wasn't in affirmations themselves. They were just misunderstood, mistaught, and misused. I eventually narrowed the flaws down to two, which enabled me to completely change my approach and design affirmations that were practical and actionable and consistently produced tangible, measurable results.

In the following pages, I'm going to give you a step-by-step formula to create Miracle Equation Affirmations that are rooted in truth and strategically designed to accelerate your application of the Miracle Equation. But before we get to that, let's take a moment to explore those two flaws and the problems they create.

## 1. Untrue Statements Make You Feel Inauthentic

We all want to improve some area of our life or our life as a whole. We want money, love, a healthy body, and maybe throw in a twenty-fifth hour of the day. We can access (almost!) all of these things with Unwavering Faith and Extraordinary Effort. We can't access them, though, by lying to ourselves. And that's how many self-help pioneers have us design our affirmations.

We've all been told to repeat phrases such as

I am successful.

I am a money magnet.

I have a perfect physique.

I am in a committed, loving relationship.

Deep down, if these statements aren't true, you know they're not true. And by repeating them, you are lying to yourself. Your subconscious will resist these lies, which leads to an additional inner conflict (as if we needed one more) and has the potential to leave you feeling worse emotionally than you did before you started. In fact, a 2009 study in *Psychological Science* revealed that people with low self-esteem actually felt worse after repeating a statement such as "I am a lovable person."* Think about it: if you believe (whether it is true or not) that you are *not* a lovable person, simply repeating that statement over and over will only pile "liar" on top of your already negative self-image.

---

* Joanne V. Wood, W. Q. Elaine Perunovic, and John W. Lee, "Positive Self Statements: Power for Some, Peril for Others," *Psychological Science* 20, no. 7 (2009): 860–66, https://doi.org/10.1111/j.1467-9280.2009.02370.x.

This type of affirmation has the potential to further chip away at the trust you have in yourself, which is counterproductive to your progress toward stepping into your new identity as a Miracle Maven. Although such hollow statements might alleviate stress and anxiety in the moment, they will hold you back from achieving what you ultimately want. The truth—your truth—will always prevail.

## 2. Passive Language Deters You from Taking Action

One of the greatest hurdles that people face when they want to improve their life is *What should I do first/next?* They become paralyzed because they can't figure out the sequence of actions to take. And so they stand still until they eventually give up. Most affirmations support this lack of action by using passive language. They gloss over the fact that you have to actually do something. Like that magical vision board hanging on your wall, they imply that you can simply attract what you want without having to do anything.

*Money will simply flow to you. The love of your life is waiting just outside your front door.* Wouldn't that be great? We would all be able to create miracles from the comfort of our La-Z-Boy recliners. Sign me up! But that isn't how life works. We don't have money trees sprouting up in our backyards. And I'm not sure about you, but if some stranger was lurking around my front door, I would call the cops (after I made sure it wasn't a delivery from Amazon Prime, of course). These types of affirmations are also lies. We do need to do something, something very specific, to achieve our goals. Remember, every result you want in your life is preceded by a process. You need to define and implement your process. Affirm that, and now you're getting somewhere.

Before we go on to the next section and learn how to construct an effective affirmation, here are a few of my favorite quotes that articulate and reinforce the benefits of affirmations.

It's the repetition of affirmations that leads to belief. And once that belief becomes a deep conviction, things begin to happen.

—MUHAMMAD ALI

Any thought that is passed on to the subconscious often enough and convincingly enough is finally accepted.

—ROBERT COLLIER,
SELF-HELP AUTHOR AND PUBLISHER

Affirmations are statements going beyond the reality of the present into the creation of the future through the words you use in the now.

—LOUISE L. HAY, AUTHOR, PUBLISHER,
AND FOUNDER OF HAY HOUSE

You've got to win in your mind before you win in your life.

—JOHN ADDISON,
LEADERSHIP SPEAKER AND AUTHOR

## FIVE SIMPLE STEPS TO CREATE AND IMPLEMENT YOUR MIRACLE EQUATION AFFIRMATIONS

As you now know, it's important that your affirmations are rooted in truth and clearly state the specific actions that are necessary to achieving whatever miracle you're ready to create. If you are priming your brain for a new reality, you also have to prime it for what you will be doing in that new reality.

## AFFIRMATIONS IN ACTION

Miranda Mart, a member of the Miracle Morning Community Facebook group, is a great example of how affirmations can change your life.

Miranda was introduced to the *Miracle Morning* book three years ago. She had just gotten divorced and was now a single mother to two young children. She was also starting a new career, on full commission, and wanted to start an agency in an industry she had zero experience in. She was depressed, was experiencing social anxiety, and had over $150,000 in bills that she had to pay on her own. Life seemed like one insurmountable hurdle in front of another.

She made her first priority her Miracle Morning routine. She reread the book every three months and did affirmations, visualizations, and scribing every day. She divided her affirmations up into three categories and saw that the more skilled she became at using affirmations, the better she was able to control her thoughts. The demons no longer controlled her.

With her daily practice, she eventually made it to being the top female producer in her entire company, among more than one thousand salespeople, and started her own agency. But she wasn't done. She continued with her affirmations and has since developed six agencies underneath her, quadrupled her income, and hit the top contract level in her company. She credits her Miracle Morning, and specifically her affirmations, with her extraordinary success.

Keep in mind that it's also important that your affirmations do not combat your current belief system. Instead, they should align, evolve, and expand it while overriding your fears. You want to gently open your mind to new possibilities so that your brain will believe them, and that means that you need to use logic, rooted in truth, combined with your predetermined process to move you toward tangible results.

Your Miracle Equation Affirmations enable you to step into an upgraded identity by determining, articulating, and reinforcing the beliefs and behaviors that align with your Miracle Maven identity. They are designed to actively program your subconscious mind with Unwavering Faith while directing your conscious mind to put forth the Extraordinary Effort necessary to create tangible, measurable results.

In summary, Miracle Equation Affirmations will accomplish two outcomes:

- Upgrade and reprogram your **subconscious mind** by minimizing or eliminating any inherent conflicts that are holding you back while actively instilling the Unwavering Faith you need to accomplish anything that you choose

- Direct your **conscious mind** toward the activities that you deem to be most important and keep you engaged in the Extraordinary Effort necessary to move your biggest goals from possible to probable to inevitable

Now let's move on to the step-by-step process you will use to create and implement practical, results-oriented Miracle Equation Affirmations that will prime your mind to create tangible, measurable miracles.

**STEP 1:** Begin with your Miracle Mantra.

Remember in chapter 7, you had the opportunity to create your Miracle Mantra, a single sentence that encapsulates your commitment to your mission and to maintaining Unwavering Faith and putting forth Extraordinary Effort—over an extended period of time—until you make your miracle a reality.

Your Miracle Mantra still stands alone as a primary tool for you to implement and maintain the Miracle Equation, and it's also important to incorporate it into your affirmations. The more you repeat something to yourself, the more deeply engrained it becomes.

> **ACTION:** Grab your journal or smartphone or open your favorite word-processing program and begin your written affirmations with your Miracle Mantra.

> **TEMPLATE:** *I am committed to maintaining Unwavering Faith that I will _____ [insert your mission from chapter 6], and I will continue putting forth Extraordinary Effort until I do, no matter what . . . there is no other option.*

**STEP 2:** Articulate why your mission is deeply meaningful.

Remember, your mission does not have to be world changing, although it certainly can be. It can be as big or small, as easy or complicated, as you like. The key is that it must be meaningful to you. That significance—your *why*—will serve as your driver, and that is why it is crucial to remind yourself of it every day, which your affirmations will do for you.

The missing link between wanting something and attaining it is often leverage, and your deeply meaningful why will give you that leverage. As my good friend Jon Vroman often says, "When your why has heart, your how gets legs." We often set goals because we want to achieve or improve something, but as soon as the pursuit of that achievement or improvement gets difficult, it is our why (or lack of) that we fall back on. If our why is weak, or worse, if we're not even clear on why we're working toward a goal, then we can easily give up. If, on the other hand, our why is highly significant—if it means more to us than anything else in the world—then we will push through any challenge and do whatever it takes to reach our goal(s), no matter what . . . there is no other option.

**ACTION:** Articulate why your mission is deeply meaningful *to you*. Your deeply meaningful why is the reason (or reasons) that you're committed to your mission and committed to staying committed *until* your mission becomes your reality. Your deeply meaningful why is the most significant benefit (or benefits) that you'll experience both through your pursuit and attainment of the mission. It could be the intangible benefit of *who you become* or a more tangible benefit such as a monetary reward, a repaired relationship, or pounds shed.

**TEMPLATE:** *The reason(s) I am committed to my mission is because [insert your deeply meaningful why—the most significant benefit(s) you'll experience by pursuing and/or attaining your mission].*

**STEP 3:** Solidify your Extraordinary Effort and make the attainment of your mission inevitable by committing to your process (without being emotionally attached to your results).

This step helps to alleviate your anxiety about the very common concern *How on earth am I going to accomplish this?* It also provides the logic your brain needs to believe that your goal is achievable and sets your expectation for your Extraordinary Effort. Consider this step as your bridge from desire to creation.

> **ACTION:** Write down your process, the one that is made up of the primary action step(s) that you've determined will be necessary to accomplish your mission, and be sure to include *when* you're committed to taking those actions. Make this as clear and concise as possible. Ideally, you will do only one measurable action consistently to avoid overwhelming yourself. Also, be sure to include how often and when you will complete your process every day.

> **TEMPLATE:** *To ensure that the attainment of my mission is inevitable, I will remain committed to my process of _____ [insert your process] on _____ [dates and times] without being emotionally attached to my results.*

**STEP 4:** Establish your Enlightened Entitlement.

Remember, Miracle Mavens live with the mindset that they *can* achieve anything that they want, *will* achieve anything that they are committed to, and that they *deserve* everything they're willing to work for. Developing the qualities of a Miracle Maven includes generating feelings of deservedness, which will fuel your Unwavering Faith and, in turn, your Extraordinary Effort. Your Miracle Equation Affirmations will begin by helping you to establish and reinforce your Enlightened Entitlement so that you feel authentically deserving of anything and everything you want for your life.

**ACTION:** Remind yourself of the universal truth that you are just as worthy, deserving, and capable of achieving everything you want (and are committed to) as any other person on Earth.

**TEMPLATE:** *I am committed to my mission and living every day as a Miracle Maven because I know that I am just as worthy, deserving, and capable of creating tangible, measurable miracles and achieving everything that I want, as any other person on Earth.*

You can copy this word for word or modify it as you'd like. Keep in mind that we all respond differently to various words and phrases, based on what resonates with us, so it's important to be mindful about the language you use. It should stimulate and resonate with you. And the same goes for each of the steps listed. For example, if referring to yourself as a Miracle Maven feels weird, that's okay (although it always feels weird, at first, to speak about yourself differently). You could replace that language with "I am committed to living every day as the best version of myself." You could also replace "everything I want" with "the life of my dreams" or replace "miracles" with "results." Again, use language that resonates with you.

## STEP 5: Recite your Miracle Equation Affirmations (with emotion). Every. Single. Day.

So many people don't stay committed to this step, which is arguably the most important of them all. They spend a fair amount of time designing their affirmations so that the words capture their upgraded identity, their mission, and their process, and then they don't stick with it—the same way people don't stick with a diet or a New Year's resolution. It's human nature. Once the initial excitement or "newness" wears off, we're tempted to divert our focus onto something else that's newer and more stimulating. This is often our downfall.

The key to creating miracles is consistency. You have to stay committed as long as it takes you to get to the place in your life where you've always wanted to be. And there is no easier way to kick off that journey than to commit to reciting your Miracle Equation Affirmations every day. Going one step further, it's also wise to recite our affirmations with some emotion. This helps your brain to match your mood in the present with your desired mood. You're not lying to yourself; you're simply showing your brain what you want to feel more often. You have to "get it" completely.

Though we may get something *intellectually*, we don't really get it until we get it *emotionally* also. As in we go from understanding it conceptually or logically to actually *feeling* the emotion. For example, when your significant other complains to you about something that is bothering him or her (and I'm speaking as a man here), though we may hear what the other person is saying and understand it intellectually, we don't always get it. If that same person starts sobbing and you can see, hear, and sometimes even feel his or her pain, you "get it" on an emotional level.

So make sure that when you recite your affirmations, you feel the truth in what you're saying. When you affirm your commitment to living every day as a Miracle Maven, with Unwavering Faith and Extraordinary Effort, take a deep breath and, as you inhale, feel your new identity wash over you. Think about what it would look like, sound like, and feel like. This will help you to experience your new identity both intellectually and emotionally.

**ACTION:** Consistency is key with the Miracle Equation, and that begins with reciting your affirmations every day to maintain and expand your limitless mindset, while also keeping you focused on your process. I find it best to have a consistent time to recite your Miracle Equation Affirmations. It can be every night before bed, in the morning after you brush your teeth, or during your Miracle Morning, when you do your personal development practice at the start of the day. Just make it part of your daily routine. And remember to feel the truth of what you're reciting. If you can, stay in that feeling as long as possible. Personally, I like to meditate directly after I recite my affirmations and use that time to fully absorb the mindset and emotions that they created. Doing this will deepen the impact that your Miracle Equation affirmations have in your life.

**DOWNLOADABLE RESOURCE:** If you'd like to download the Miracle Equation Affirmations one-page template, which incorporates all of these steps, visit www.tmebonuses.com.

## MIRACLE EQUATION AFFIRMATIONS

1.  I am committed to maintaining Unwavering Faith that I will [insert your mission from chapter 6], and I will continue putting forth Extraordinary Effort until I do, no matter what . . . there is no other option.

2.  The reason(s) I am committed to my mission is because [insert your deeply meaningful why—the most significant benefit(s) you'll experience by pursuing and/or attaining your mission].

3.  To ensure that the attainment of my mission is inevitable, I will remain committed to my process of _____ [insert your process] on _____ [date and time], without being emotionally attached to my results.

4.  I am committed to my mission and living every day as a Miracle Maven, because I know that I am just as worthy, deserving, and capable of creating miracles and achieving everything I want as any other person on Earth.

**PERSONAL EXAMPLE:** I'm about to share my current version of one of my Miracle Equation Affirmations with you. You'll notice some of the wording is slightly different from the template, because as I mentioned a few pages ago, it's important to use language that resonates with you. I'm constantly editing and updating my affirmations as I continue to learn, grow, and gain new perspectives:

1.  I am committed to maintaining Unwavering Faith that I will stay cancer-free and live a long, healthy life (to be one

hundred years old, when Sophie will be seventy and Halsten will be sixty-seven), and I will continue putting forth Extraordinary Effort every day, for the rest of my life, no matter what . . . there is no other option.

2. The reason(s) I am committed to my mission is because being alive to positively influence Sophie and Halsten and share my life with Ursula means more to me than anything else in the world.

3. To ensure that I live a long, healthy, one-hundred-plus-year life, I will remain committed to my process of following all of my (daily) holistic anti-cancer protocols combined with my allopathic treatments, to maximize the life-saving benefits of both.

4. I am committed to my mission and living every day as a Miracle Maven because I know that I am just as worthy, deserving, and capable of living a long, healthy, one-hundred-plus-year life, alongside my family, as any other person on Earth.

## EVOLVE YOUR AFFIRMATIONS OVER TIME

Edit and update your affirmations as needed, to keep up with your ever-evolving identity and goals. As you grow and evolve, so should your affirmations. And as you succeed in creating tangible, measurable miracles, you'll have to develop new affirmations for your new goals and missions. In time, developing your affirmations will come to be almost second nature. Through experience, you'll know what to write, what works best for you, and how to use your affirmations to maintain your Unwavering Faith and Extraordinary Effort toward each new goal that emerges.

Realistically, we all have a lot of reprogramming to do. We have many years of limiting beliefs and internal conflicts to unravel and fears to overcome. Eventually I recommend writing affirmations for each area of your life, which may also include specific goals, and they will change depending on what you want to focus on at that particular time. Some mornings, I'll read all of my affirmations. Other times, I'll read the ones that I feel are most pressing. If I happen to be working toward one specific mission, I make sure that I read that one until my mission is complete.

Here is a list of my foundational affirmation topics, each of which I have goals in:

- My health and fitness (including remaining free from cancer)
- My mission and purpose
- My wife
- My children
- Extended family
- Friends
- Income and financial freedom
- Personal development
- Spirituality
- Contribution

Also, know that there are infinite ways to word or structure affirmations, and I use many variations for different purposes. The step-by-step formula we just went through is specific to implementing the Miracle Equation. In their simplest form, affirmations are merely reminders of what matters most to you. A reminder might be of an important goal, a daily action, an empowering feeling, a fundamental mindset, a value, a purpose, or anything else you want to keep at the forefront of your mind. I'm sure you've heard the saying that what you focus on expands. Affirmations will help you ensure that you are always focused on and expanding in the areas that are most important to you.

For example, one of my affirmations reads, "I will do something today to make my wife's life amazing." By reading that every morning, I'm reminded to be proactive and to do at least one thing that adds value for my wife every single day. It usually involves something simple such as doing the dishes, buying her flowers, telling her how much I love her, letting her sleep in, or taking some task off of her plate to make her day a little easier. Sometimes it's a bit grander, such as planning a vacation or surprising her by taking our kids somewhere and giving her a day of solitude. Whatever it is, my daily practice of reading my affirmations reminds me to take a single action that adds some sort of value to my wife's life. You know what they say: "Happy wife, happy life."

Though your goals and mission will change over time, your identity as a Miracle Maven should not—not if you want to continue creating miracles. You will consistently have to choose Unwavering Faith and Extraordinary Effort. You will consistently have to fight your internal conflict to remember how powerful you really are. You will consistently have to stay present to why your goals are deeply meaningful to you. Affirmations, in the way that you've just learned, will support you in accomplishing all of this. And they only require a few minutes of your focused attention each day.

Now that you know exactly how to create and use your Miracle Equation affirmations (make sure that you schedule time to create them or download the template), it's time to pull together everything you've learned to this point and try it out. In the next chapter, I'll be inviting you to participate in your first 30-day Miracle Equation challenge. As my first coach used to say, "This is where the rubber meets the road!"

**Note:** If you have questions or want help or feedback while writing your Miracle Equation Affirmations, feel free to post them in the Miracle Morning Community at www.mytmmcommunity.com. There you will find 150,000-plus like-minded individuals who are already practicing these types of daily affirmations, supporting one another, and will be more than happy to support you.

10

# THE MIRACLE EQUATION 30-DAY CHALLENGE

It's Time for Your First Mission

Be willing to be uncomfortable.
Be comfortable being uncomfortable.
It may get tough, but it's a small price to
pay for living a dream.

—PETER MCWILLIAMS, AUTHOR

magine that you have reached the end of your life, and it's your last day on Earth. Your accomplishments are already behind you. There is nothing left to do—no more time for growth, personal development, or pursuing goals. You have done everything that you will ever do in this lifetime.

Now let's further suspend reality and imagine that the person you could have become—the version of you living at your full potential—walks into the room. Not surprisingly, you feel as though you've known this person for your entire life, and you feel totally at ease. You chat a little with each other, just enough for you to get a feel for what this Level 10 version of you is like: his or her mindset, accomplishments, contributions, and level of fulfillment. This version of you lived life to the fullest, gave it everything he or she had, reaped the rewards, and is leaving this lifetime as fulfilled as any person could be.

Now, based on your current trajectory, do you think these two versions of yourself would be pretty similar or far apart?

It's a heavy question, but if you are honest with yourself, it's an excellent way to measure how fulfilling and productive your life currently is and can be. One of the saddest things is to go through life knowing that you're not achieving and/or contributing all that you can. Yet so many of us fall into this trap. Even if you are already highly successful in one or more areas of your life, there's a strong likelihood that there are opportunities for you to apply more of your potential in other areas.

This final chapter gives you the opportunity to put everything you've learned from this book into practice so that you can move closer to that Level 10 version of yourself. In one month's time, the Miracle Equation will become so deeply ingrained in your consciousness that you won't have to make a conscious effort to think about it again. It will become part of who you are. Unwavering Faith will become your default mindset. Extraordinary Effort will feel ordinary.

The next thirty days will be a simple but transformative journey that will end in your embodying the identity of a Miracle Maven who can create tangible, measurable miracles in all areas of your life.

## THE MOST COMMON OBSTACLES YOU WILL FACE AND HOW TO OVERCOME THEM

As you know, I want to make your path to living as a Miracle Maven as easy as possible. Making things more difficult than they need to be (which is almost always done in our minds) is unproductive and unnecessary. So I want to address the most common obstacles now, so that you'll be prepared for them and know how to move past them if (or when) they come up.

The first obstacle that usually rears one of its many heads is our *irrational fears*—fear of failure, fear of success, fear of change—which usually cause us to procrastinate. Know that everyone experiences fear and trepidation when they first set out toward a significant goal. Anytime we dare to venture outside the cozy confines of our comfort zone, it's uncomfortable. Tackling something important to you, especially if you have never done anything like it before, is scary. Having such feelings is normal and expected.

What we want to do, though, is move you through that part of the process quickly and seamlessly. If you catch your brain slipping back into its default stress response and thinking negative thoughts about your goal or yourself, take a deep breath and recite your Miracle Mantra to refocus your attention on what's possible and what you're committed to, rather than what you're afraid of. Remember, you are in control of your thoughts and, in turn, your reality. Reciting your Miracle Equation Affirmations daily (which will be one of your steps in the 30-Day Challenge) will likewise give your brain space to release your fears and instead focus on what you're committed to and why you're committed to it.

If you still feel afraid or stuck, I invite you to refer back to chapter 3 and see if you can identify whether you are experiencing any of the four inherent conflicts:

- The irrational fear of opportunity versus maintaining the status quo: *Do you fear opportunities?*

- Misdirected Entitlement versus Enlightened Entitlement: *Do you feel undeserving?*

- Potential Dysmorphia versus actualized potential: *Do you not see your true capabilities?*

- The world defines you versus you define you: *Do you allow others to limit you?*

Understanding what is holding you back is the first step toward overcoming it.

Another obstacle that I have seen over and over again with clients and friends who have taken on this challenge is how to handle emotional attachment to short-term results. Remember my friend who was following through with his process to lose weight (restricting calories and exercising daily), but the numbers on the scale just wouldn't budge? His emotional attachment almost caused him to quit, until he realized that he was maintaining his weight while reducing his body fat percentage. His effort was paying off.

Consider how long I put forth Extraordinary Effort to promote *The Miracle Morning* before I saw any significant increase in sales. I remained committed to my process by being a guest on more than one hundred podcasts, publishing over fifty of my own podcast episodes, appearing on a dozen morning television shows, and much more before sales of the book finally took off. If I had been emotionally attached to my short-term results (which were mediocre), I would have given up in month two . . . or four . . . or twelve . . . and definitely wouldn't have made it to month eighteen. Luckily, I understood that if there is any real secret of success, it's this: *Stay committed to your process without being emotionally attached to your results.* Every result is preceded by a process, and as long as you stay committed to that process over an extended period of time, your success will eventually become inevitable.

Another obstacle is *impatience*. We live in a time and culture of immediate gratification. We can contact friends instantly via text message. We can access any kind of media that strikes our fancy at a particular moment with a few simple swipes on our phone. We can even order new shoes or groceries for delivery the same day. The value of patience, it seems, is going by the wayside.

But when it comes to creating miracles, patience is a crucial component. Some miracles just take longer to achieve. If you set out to write a book, for example, it's not going to happen in an afternoon (unless it's a really short book). It will take persistence, even if you have calculated how many words you need to write each day to finish by a certain date. Every book I've written, including this one, took longer than I had originally anticipated. My first book took me six years to write. My second took me three years. This one took me six months (after I told my publisher I'd have it done in three).

Impatience will cause your stress level to spike and make it harder for you to stay committed to your process. Impatience will zap your creativity, hinder your ability to focus, and cloud any problem-solving mojo you may need to engage along the way. If you find yourself tapping your foot impatiently and getting worked up about not having achieved your goal yet, remember that you're in this for the long haul and that this is a way of living.

Now that you're armed with the strategies and information you need to overcome some of the common obstacles to becoming a Miracle Maven, let's jump into the 30-Day Challenge itself.

## YOUR MIRACLE EQUATION 30-DAY CHALLENGE

**DOWNLOADABLE RESOURCE:** For a downloadable Miracle Equation 30-Day Challenge workbook, visit www.tmebonuses.com.

The Miracle Equation 30-Day Challenge consists of six steps, three of which you may have already completed while working your way through this book. If that's the case, congratulations; you are halfway through your challenge already! If you didn't take the time to do the first three steps while you were reading because you got so excited that you just kept reading (I wouldn't fault you for that, because I do it all the time!), I would encourage you to review the steps below and then go back and revisit that corresponding chapter so that you can complete each step now.

### THE 30-DAY CHALLENGE IN ACTION

As full disclosure, this is the first time that the Miracle Equation 30-Day Challenge is being introduced to the world, so I don't have a bunch of examples to share with you. However, the Miracle Equation 30-Day Challenge was modeled upon the Miracle Morning 30-Day Challenge, which has now been implemented by hundreds of thousands of people all around the world. And the results have been astounding.

In just thirty days, here is what Dawn Pogue from Ontario, Canada, accomplished:

- She quit smoking (30 days smoke free)
- She exercised every day (30 days of elliptical training)
- She quit caffeine (30 days no coffee)
- She got into shape (lost 11 pounds and 42 inches)
- She rebuilt her confidence

Gillian Perkins from Salem, Oregon, was able to

- Read three books
- Grow her business by 30 percent
- Save $5,000 toward the down payment on her next home
- Work out three times a week
- Lower her body fat percentage from 36 percent to 23 percent
- Start writing her first book
- Completely organize and deep clean her entire house

Georgios Griorakis from Cologne, Germany, also accomplished a lot. He

- Prepared and published three articles on his blog
- Ran a half marathon
- Consistently followed a careful nutrition program
- Listened to more than twenty podcasts while exercising
- Increased his confidence, persistence, and self-discipline and in general felt proud to have successfully and consistently completed the 30-Day Challenge

This just goes to show you how significantly you can change your life in only thirty days. Now it's your turn.

### STEP 1: Determine your first mission.

Remember in chapter 6 when I shared the story of my committing to a mission of running a fifty-two-mile ultramarathon because I hated running and I wanted to meet the guy—to *become* the guy—who could pull it off? Now it's your turn. What is *your* ultramarathon? As in what mission is so far outside of your comfort zone that you don't even know the person you would need to be to achieve it, but you'd love to meet him or her and become that person?

To decide on your mission, simply look over all of your goals and ask yourself: *Which one of these goals will enable me to become the person that I need to be to achieve everything else I want for my life?* The answer to that question is your mission.

You want your mission to both motivate and energize you, but it also may intimidate/scare you a little—or a lot. You want it to be significant enough to move you out of your current way of living and challenging enough to stretch you into the next level of your abilities. Make sure you've considered your values and what matters most to you, as your mission should be deeply meaningful. Then determine a tangible, measurable miracle that reflects the value that you would like to amplify in your life right now. This will be your first mission.

### STEP 2: Predetermine your process.

Having clarity energizes us. When we know exactly what to do next and we know that doing it will move us closer to where we ultimately want to go, the prospect of inevitable success fuels our motivation. Remember to keep your process as simple and actionable as possible.

Doing one task at a time is usually best. If you don't yet know what your process should be, your initial process will be researching and figuring out what your process is going to be. Search for free articles on Google related to your mission. Search Amazon for the highest-rated books on your topic. If your mission involves developing an ability, mastering a skill, or becoming an expert on a topic, your initial process may be practicing and/or learning. Remember, this is a way of living.

Russell Simmons stated in his book *Do You!: 12 Laws to Access the Power in You to Achieve Happiness and Success*, "I know some people say 'Keep your eyes on the prize,' but I disagree. When your eyes are stuck on the prize, you're going to keep stumbling and crashing into things. If you really want to get ahead, you've got to keep your eyes focused on the path." In this context, the path is your process. Remember that every result is preceded by a process and the key to consistent goal achievement is to *stay committed to your process without being emotionally attached to your results.*

## STEP 3: Schedule time to recite your Miracle Equation Affirmations. Every. Single. Day.

Remember, it is only through consistent (daily) repetition that we are going to open our minds to new possibilities. You can't recite an affirmation once, or even ten times, and expect it to transform your thinking. It's like exercising; you have to do it consistently and over a long period of time to reap the rewards. To replace your fear with faith and to ensure that your faith remains unwavering, you'll need to reinforce it every day. So pull out your schedule right now, and create a recurring appointment with yourself to recite your affirmations. This step should take you only a few minutes, and you'll be on your way.

**STEP 4:** Schedule your process and be held accountable to it.

Extraordinary Effort is all about *consistency*. It's about implementing your predetermined process and doing at least one thing each day that moves you closer to the attainment of your mission. I have a recurring sixty-minute appointment in my schedule each morning labeled "Mission Time" to ensure I make progress on my top priority before I do anything else. Maybe for you it'll be thirty or sixty minutes, five to seven days a week, in the morning or evening, before or after work. Or it could be four hours on Saturday and four hours on Sunday, before you spend time with your family or relaxing by yourself. Be sure to schedule your process when you are at your best, when your energy and ability to focus are at their peak. For me that's in the morning. I get kinda brain dead in the afternoon.

Before leaving this step, check in with the person or people in your life who are going to hold you accountable to share your commitment with them and establish how they will keep you on track (with daily or weekly check-ins) and your mode of communication. This is where your commitment begins to take hold, so be thoughtful with this step and make sure that the time you schedule is reasonable and consistent.

**STEP 5:** Assess your process and your progress daily.

While you don't want to be emotionally attached to your short-term results, you definitely want to be aware of them. Sometimes we need to modify our process as we go along. Other times, it's helpful to reflect on our progress. I recommend implementing a daily *scribing* practice to keep you aware of your mission and keep your momentum rolling. Some folks like to do this in the morning to reflect on the day before, while others prefer to scribe at night after that day's activities. Consider what would be most effective for you.

Some questions to start you off could be

1. What was my biggest win in the last twenty-four hours?

2. Did I follow through with my process?

3. What was my biggest area of improvement?

4. Is there anything I could have done differently or better?

5. What lessons have I learned so far?

6. Do I need to make any changes or adjustments to my process?

7. Is there anyone else I can reach out to for advice or feedback?

**DOWNLOADABLE RESOURCE:** The questions listed above (and many more) are included in the Miracle Equation 30-Day Challenge workbook at www.tmebonuses.com.

**STEP 6:** Evaluate your experience at the completion of each mission.

One common trait among successful individuals and teams is that they take time after completing a project to reflect on lessons learned that they can use moving forward. As you know, each of your goals is important, but the greatest value that you can capture from your goals is the qualities and characteristics that you develop (i.e., who you become) during that process. Capturing and then integrating what you learn along the way toward your goal is paramount to becoming a Miracle Maven.

Here are some more questions to get you started.

1. Did I reach my goal?

2. Is there anything I could have done differently or better?

3. What did I learn from this?

4. What changes will I make for my next Miracle Mission?

## BEFORE YOU GO . . .

As you gear up for your first mission, know that you already have everything you need to live every day as a Miracle Maven and create the most extraordinary life you can imagine. Actually, you've always had the abilities within you; I've simply attempted to shine a spotlight on them. I hope you have learned what you needed to learn during our time together, and I wish you great success on your first mission and those that will follow. Now there are only two decisions standing between you and moving your biggest goals from possible . . . to probable . . . to inevitable. It's time to start creating miracles.

# WHAT WILL YOU DO NOW?

Now this is not the end.

It is not even the beginning of the end.

But it is, perhaps,

the end of the beginning.

—WINSTON CHURCHILL

We've covered a lot of material during our time together, and I want to both acknowledge and thank you for getting to the end with me, which, of course, is much closer to the beginning of your journey. I have tried to deconstruct miracles in a way that will show you how practical and realistic they are to achieve. Despite what many people think and even what you may have thought when you first picked this book up, there's nothing mysterious about miracles—at least not the types of tangible, measurable miracles that you will be actively identifying and creating.

By following the Miracle Equation and using the additional strategies we've talked about, creating miracles over and over again will become your way of life. As long as you maintain the two decisions we've explored in this book, your success will be inevitable, and you will find that anything you want is possible. I know that's a big promise to make, but I have seen it too many times to believe otherwise.

I have been blessed with opportunities to overcome life-threatening challenges and create the life I have always wanted through my unwavering commitment to live by the Miracle Equation for nearly two decades. I have also had the privilege of being a part of other people's miracles, watching them overcome their internal conflicts to go beyond what they once believed was impossible. Not through magic. Not by staring at a vision board. But by actively making and then maintaining the same two decisions that the world's highest achievers throughout history have made, Unwavering Faith and Extraordinary Effort.

You can have the same experience. You can create extraordinary changes in your life and do so faster than you've ever thought possible. In the next thirty days, you can overcome the fears, doubts, and internal conflicts that have held you back. You have the power within you to manifest what you may have previously deemed impossible.

There are no limits for you. The life that you want *and are willing to create* is your birthright.

With regard to moving your biggest goals from possible to probable to inevitable, know that it's not a matter of will you or won't you. Eventually you will. When you apply the Miracle Equation, the biggest variable is simply *time*, how long it will take you to achieve your mission. Things often take longer than we think or hope they will, but the rewards are always worth the effort, and worth the wait.

**Remember, anytime you find yourself wishing that you were further along than you are or comparing where you are with where someone else is, keep in mind that when you finally get to the point you've been working toward for so long, you almost never wish it had happened any sooner.** Instead, you see that the journey and the timing are perfect. The challenges and obstacles were necessary to your growth. So no matter what stage you're at now, be at peace with where you are while maintaining a healthy sense of urgency to make the consistent progress each day that will ensure that you get to wherever it is you want to go. You *will* get there, and the timing will be perfect.

If you remember from the introduction, the miracle I'm committed to achieving with this book is to *elevate the consciousness of humanity one person at a time*. Though I'm guessing that that may have caused an eye roll when you first read it, I hope that you now see how possible that mission actually is. Every day, I will continue applying the Miracle Equation to accomplish this goal until I feel that it has happened. Plain and simple. I know that over time my mission will move from possible to probable to inevitable. *There is no other option.*

So . . . what about you? Have you decided on your first mission yet? Are you gearing up for your 30-Day Challenge?

As you set out, I invite you to stretch your thinking beyond just yourself. Sure, it's great to create miracles around our individual pursuits (and these miracles are important), but don't lose sight of the bigger picture. Now that you know how to create tangible, measurable miracles, you also have a responsibility regarding which miracles you choose to create. Look out into the world around you. What's missing? What would you like to see more of? Where can you leave your unique personal mark? What will your legacy be? Yes, start with yourself and your family. But then move out into your community and grow from there. As a Miracle Maven, your potential to impact others is also limitless, and that is a responsibility that none of us should take lightly.

As you now know, living in alignment with two simple decisions will open up a new paradigm of possibility for you, and it's up to you which possibilities you commit to turning into inevitabilities. No goal or dream or mission is too big, because you cannot fail. You can only learn, grow, and become better than you've ever been before. I cannot wait to hear about the miracles you create.

# ACKNOWLEDGMENTS

If it takes a village to raise a child, it might take two to write a book. I want to express my heartfelt gratitude to the following people, who make up my village:

My wife for life and the woman of my dreams, Ursula. You are the most incredible wife, mother, and human being I could ever hope to share my life with. With your unwavering support, you make everything I do possible. My heart belongs to you, as long as you promise to share it with the following two people . . .

Our children, Sophie and Halsten. You two are my inspiration, and you both mean more to me than anything else in this world.

My parents, Mark and Julie. If I could go back to the beginning of my life and choose any set of parents, I would choose you both! I am who I am because of your unconditional love and influence.

My sister, Hayley, for always believing in me and being someone whom I deeply love and respect.

Tiffany Swineheart, my director of operations. There are no words to express both how much value you've added to my life and how much I appreciate you. You are the best, Tiff.

Jon Berghoff, my close friend and business partner. When I was in the hospital fighting cancer, you stepped up in major ways to support me and my family. I love you, Buddy.

Honorée Corder, my friend and cocreator of *The Miracle Morning* book series. When I was in the hospital fighting cancer, you also stepped up (I think you published two books in the series!) to help me and my family. I love you, HC!

John Maas and Celeste Fine, my world-class agents at Sterling Lord Literistic, for their unwavering faith and extraordinary effort in making this book a reality.

Emily Klein, for helping me to focus my ADHD brain and turning my often incoherent inspiration into coherent concepts for the readers of this book.

Diana Baroni and the team at Penguin Random House for believing in *The Miracle Equation* and bringing it to the world.

Every single member of the global Miracle Morning Community, for waking up every day to fulfill your potential and supporting one another to do the same. Together, we are truly elevating the consciousness of humanity, one morning at a time. I love you all!

# INDEX

# The Miracle Morning Series

The Miracle Morning

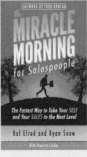

for Salespeople

for Real Estate Agents

for Addiction Recovery

for Couples

for Transforming Your Relationship

for Network Marketers

for Writers

for Parents

for Millionaires

for College Students

for Entrepreneurs